Rivers of Wales

First edition: August 1997
© Rosemary Hutton/Y Lolfa Cyf., 1997

ISBN: 0 86243 373 8

Photographs: Rosemary Hutton

Printed and published in Wales
by Y Lolfa Cyf., Talybont, Ceredigion, SY24 5HE
e-mail ylolfa@netwales.co.uk
world-wide web http://www.ylolfa.wales.com/
tel (01970) 832 304
fax 832 782

Rivers of
WALES

Rosemary Hutton

The Country Code

1. Guard against fire
2. Fasten all gates
3. Keep dogs under control
4. Keep to paths where these are clearly visible
5. Avoid damaging fences, hedges, walls
6. Pick up and take home all litter
7. Safeguard water supplies
8. Protect wildlife
9. Take care on country roads
10. Respect the life of the countryside

Contents

Key to Maps

 Rivers

 Streams

 Lakes/Reservoirs

 Canal with towpath

 Broad-leaved woods

Coniferous woods

Fresh/salt water marshes

 Embankment

 Shingle

 Rocks/quarry workings

 Castle mound

Key to Maps

	Roads/lanes
	Forestry/estate roads
	Bridge
	Footbridge
⊣⊢⊢⊣⊣⏺⊢⊢⊢⊢	Railway with station
–⊢–⊢–⊢–⊢–	Disused railway
–>– –>– –	Direction of walk
=⊣⊢⊣⊢⊣⊢=	Boardwalk
✕	Picnic site
✕ 🚐	Camping/caravan site
⸸ ✝	Church or chapel – with/without steeple
P. *i* Y.H.	Parking – Information – Youth hostel
W.C.	Public Conveniences
T. P.H.	Public telephone – Pub/inn
P.O.	Post Office
N.T. F.C.	National Trust – Forestry Commission

River
CONWY

Introduction

The countryside surrounding the River Conwy and its tributaries is today one of the most visited areas of North Wales. The river's source is a shallow lake, Llyn Conwy, in the moorland known as the Migneint. For the first few miles, the river flows in a north-easterly direction almost as far as the village of Pentrefoelas on the A5. It then takes a sharp turn to the west and begins its familiar journey to Betws-y-coed. The valley here is narrow and wooded and the Conwy is joined by several important tributaries. From Betws-y-coed to Trefriw

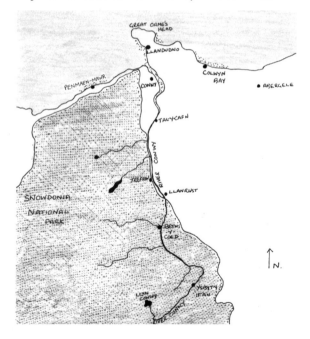

where the river becomes tidal, the valley gradually widens in the east although it is still overlooked by steep, wooded hills to the west. In addition to the railway which follows the east bank of the river there are good roads on both sides of the valley providing easy access all the way to the resorts of Conwy and Llandudno on the river's estuary.

There is plenty of varied accommodation throughout the area.

OS maps covering the River Conwy are 115, 116 and 124 in the Landranger 1:50,000 series and sheets 17 and 18 in the Outdoor Leisure 1:25,000 series (Snowdonia).

Llyn Conwy and the Migneint

Llyn Conwy is the source of the River Conwy and lies nearly 1500 feet (450 metres) up in the great expanse of moorland called the Migneint. The lake covers around 97 acres and has long been famed for the quality of its trout. It was formerly administered by the Lord of Penrhyn. Today much of the moorland surrounding it is under the guardianship of the National Trust.

The B4407 Ffestiniog to Pentrefoelas road crosses the Migneint and follows the Conwy for several miles. At Pontarconwy, near an isolated farmhouse, a track can be followed up to the lake. Just below the farmhouse there is a picturesque waterfall.

Another road crosses the moorland, this time to the

The River Conwy near its source in the Migneint

west of the river, and from here a public footpath leads across to the lake. Extreme caution is needed on this walk because of the boggy conditions; do not attempt it in mist or low cloud.

Although at first sight appearing barren and uninteresting, the Migneint is home to a variety of flora and fauna. In early spring flocks of curlews are sometimes seen looking for nesting sites. Other breeding species here include golden plovers, snipe, red grouse and lapwings. In spring also, the banks of the Conwy are dotted with the striking yellow globe-flower and in summer the moorland is covered in white cotton-grass.

Ysbyty Ifan

Approaching Ysbyty Ifan along the B4407 from Pontarconwy, you will be struck by the sudden change. The barren, treeless moorland gives way to leafy lanes and green fields as you get near the village. Under a stone bridge in the village centre, the river cascades over huge grey rocks – a marvellous sight after heavy rain or a snow melt.

The name of the village means 'the hospice of St John' and recalls the days of pilgrimage to places such as Bardsey in North Wales and St David's in Pembrokeshire. In those days, the countryside around Llyn Conwy was owned by the Knights of St John of Jerusalem and was not under the jurisdiction of the King. However, the knights were not strong enough and the district became a haven for outlaws and bandits. They were eventually defeated and dispersed by local soldiers led by members of the powerful Wynn family of Gwydir. Today this quiet village consists of a cluster of stone houses and a church on the site of the hospice.

A few miles downstream where the B4407 meets the A5, the River Conwy takes a sharp turn to the west. Just over a mile to the east, much of the village of Pentrefoelas has been designated a conservation area. A heritage trail leads visitors around some of the old village industries and crafts still in operation. The village has long been a popular 'stopping off' place on the old coaching road.

Ysbyty Ifan village

Penmachno and the Afon Machno

In these upper reaches of the River Conwy where the valley is still narrow and wooded, a major tributary joins from the south-west. This is the Afon Machno and almost the whole length of the river can be followed by

Afon Machno near the woollen-mills

road. From the B4407, turn on to the minor road at Ffynnon Eidda and the valley of the Machno is soon reached. Up near the source, the community known as Glanaber Terrace dates from the time when much of this area was quarried for slate.

Beside the river to the north, Penmachno boasts a medieval church with early Christian inscribed stones. The bridge over the Machno dates from the 18th century.

North-west of the village is Tŷ Mawr cottage. Access is by means of a minor road through forestry land. Now owned by the National Trust, this cottage was the birthplace of Bishop Morgan in 1540. He completed the first translation of the Bible into Welsh, which was published in 1588. About 1½ miles farther down the valley is a woollen-mill where visitors can watch the weaving process. Nearby, a packhorse bridge over the Afon Machno is known as the Roman Bridge. Before reaching the River Conwy, the Machno tumbles over rocks to create a series of lovely waterfalls.

Machno Walk

A very easy, short walk: may be muddy in places. About an hour should be sufficient to complete the walk.

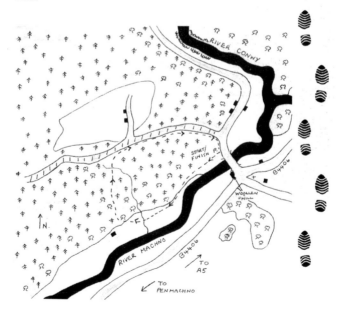

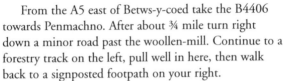

From the A5 east of Betws-y-coed take the B4406 towards Penmachno. After about ¾ mile turn right down a minor road past the woollen-mill. Continue to a forestry track on the left, pull well in here, then walk back to a signposted footpath on your right.

Go up the narrow signposted footpath into the forestry and follow the bank of the River Machno. Climb a stile then continue along this well-worn path. Cross a stream that comes in from the right and walk beside the fence. Cross the first stile on your right into the wood. Go up onto a forestry track and turn right. Continuing to bear right follow this track downhill until you reach the tarmac lane.

Conwy Falls

Near the confluence of the Machno and Conwy rivers, the B4406 from Penmachno joins the busy A5 as it continues towards Betws-y-coed. Near this junction are the famous Conwy Falls, which can be approached from the A5 where there is a parking place, viewing point and the equally famous Conwy Falls tearooms.

An alternative and quieter route is the minor road that leaves the B4406 by the woollen-mills. This follows first the Machno then the Conwy past the Falls and on to the Fairy Glen – another popular attraction.

There the river flows through a steep, narrow gorge. Care should be taken if you wish to get a closer look at the river. There are some slippery, rocky paths giving good views of the Falls. Along this lane you will notice signs on trees beside the gorge stating that no canoeing is allowed on this stretch of river – proof that this is 'white water' country.

Beyond the Fairy Glen you can either cross the Afon Lledr to join the A470 west of Betws-y-coed or continue in a westerly direction along a narrow lane. The lane soon turns south and will bring you eventually to Tŷ Mawr cottage and then back down to Penmachno. However this road is not recommended for those who dislike narrow, unfenced lanes.

The Afon Lledr, which joins the Conwy 1 mile south of Betws-y-coed, is another important tributary. It flows through one of North Wales's most beautiful valleys whose attractions include Dolwyddelan Castle, perched on a hilltop above the A470 Blaenau Ffestiniog road.

River Conwy near the Fairy Glen

Betws-y-coed (1)

The name Betws-y-coed means the 'Prayer house in the wood'. Near a peaceful stretch of the River Conwy, by the suspension bridge, is the church of St Michael and All Angels. It is of 14th century origin but is

St Mary's church,
Betws-y-coed

believed to be on the site of a much earlier building. It is surrounded by ancient yews and in the churchyard there are gravestones dating back to the late 17th century. Inside the church, the wooden altar dates from the same period and there is stained glass from the 15th and 16th centuries.

Overlooking the park is St Mary's church where services were first held in 1873. Behind the church, the wooded hills rise steeply and a footpath leads high up into the forest.

Betws-y-coed's excellent visitors' centre is housed in the former stables of the nearby Royal Oak Hotel.

It was in the early 19th century, following a visit by the artist, David Cox, that Betws-y-coed first became widely known as a beauty spot. He immortalised it and the surrounding countryside in paintings during his tour of North Wales in 1905/6.

Today the area is a Mecca for tourists from all over the world. The town centre car-parks are often full to bursting with coaches bringing thousands of visitors keen to explore some of the area's many attractions, which include hill, forest and riverside walks.

Betws-y-coed (2)

In 1868 a railway link was completed from Llandudno Junction to Betws-y-coed and since then the town has enjoyed enormous popularity as one of Wales's most famous resorts. Most of the major attractions in and around the towns are natural features enhanced by some creative architecture.

Near the town centre and spanning the Afon Llugwy is Pont y Pair or 'Bridge of the Cauldron'. It takes its name from the swirling white water of the river as it crashes over huge boulders and around the aptly named Fir Tree Island. The bridge was designed by Howell, the mason from Bala, who died in the second half of the 15th century.

On the southern outskirts of the town and carrying the A5 across the River Conwy is Thomas Telford's cast iron Waterloo Bridge. It was completed in 1815 and commemorates the battle of the same name, which was fought in

Shopping and entertainment behind Betws-y-coed station

that year. It is decorated with the emblems of the British Isles – leek, rose, shamrock and thistle.

A very different and unusual bridge spans the Llugwy near Pentre-du just to the west of Betws-y-coed. This is the Miners' Bridge and consists of a wooden walkway or gangplank. It was built for the men who worked the lead mines in the hills to the north. Today a public footpath crosses the bridge to link waymarked woodland trails both north and south of the river.

Betws-y-coed Walk

An easy, mostly level walk. Paths may be muddy. Allow about 2 hours.

Park in one of two lay-bys just outside Betws-y-coed on the A470 to Llanrwst. Walk on the verge towards Llanrwst until you reach a footpath sign on your left. Go down the track and continue towards the farm. Before reaching the farm go through a gap between a wall and a fence, then follow the hard-core track around keeping the buildings on your left. Go through a small wooden gate and follow a tarmac path to the suspension bridge over the River Conwy. Go over the bridge and onto the lane, then turn right into St Michael's churchyard. Follow the outer churchyard wall round above the river then go out onto the lane and walk straight ahead. When the lane peters out continue straight ahead down the path above the river. Go through a wicket gate onto the golf-course. Now follow the river bank around the golf-course. After about ½ mile the River Llugwy joins the Conwy. Keeping the

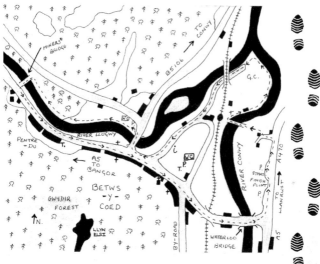

river on your right follow the bank until you reach a
gate in front of you. Go through the gate and up the
path still keeping to the river. Continue along this path,
under the railway bridge and past the waterworks. The
path now becomes a track and you should follow it past
some houses, a car-park and the visitors' centre and out
onto the main road. Turn right, then first right over
Pont y Pair (B5106 Trefriw) and then go immediately
left down the path towards the riverbank. Continue
along this waymarked path, which occasionally climbs
above the river, until you reach a path on your left down
to the Miners' Bridge. Cross the bridge and follow the
footpath onto the main road. Turn left and follow this
road back through Betws-y-coed; go over Waterloo
Bridge then turn left onto the A470 to Llanrwst. Walk
back to the parking place.

Gwydir Forest

Well known and enjoyed by thousands of walkers and picnickers is Gwydir Forest. It covers around 23 square miles (60 square kms) to the south, north and west of Betws-y-coed.

Originally this woodland was part of the Gwydir estate belonging to the Wynn family who lived at Gwydir Castle near Llanrwst. During the First World War timber was desperately needed because less was being imported. In common with many other areas of Britain, large tracts of these ancient woods were felled, and the trees carted off to sawmills near Betws-y-coed and thence to other destinations by rail.

Gwydir Uchaf chapel

In the 1920s the Forestry Commission took over the management of the forest and began planting these uplands with fast-growing conifers. Although dismissed by some for its lack of conservation interest, the forest does provide a valuable recreation facility for the hoards of visitors that descend on this part of North Wales – leaving the more sensitive areas relatively free from human disturbance. Throughout the forest there are many waymarked trails, parking and picnic sites, and the Forestry Commission allows pedestrian access to most of its woods and forests unless signs state otherwise.

Despite the seemingly overwhelming presence of 'foreign' trees there are still some marvellous examples of the old forest remaining. Towering beech and oak trees, well over 200 years old, can be seen near the Gwydir Uchaf chapel (where the Commission has a visitors' centre) and also in the woods near the Penmachno woollen-mill.

Llanrwst

The old market town of Llanrwst lies on the east bank of the Conwy where the valley begins to widen and the river flows more sedately on its journey north.

Good road and rail links make this a popular place for visitors and, in addition to the many hotels and guest-houses in the town, there are several caravan and camping sites nearby. Livestock markets are held on Wednesdays and Fridays, and a general market on Tuesday makes for a lively town centre at any time of year.

The parish church is dedicated to St Grwst and is a fine building containing a carved rood screen brought here from the now ruined Maenan Abbey north of the town. In the 17th century the Wynns of Gwydir Castle built a chapel onto the side of the church. It contains many interesting tombs and brasses and a stone coffin believed to be that of Llywelyn ap Iorwerth –

The 17th century bridge over the Conwy at Llanrwst

Llywelyn the Great, Prince of Gwynedd.

One of Llanrwst's most popular features is the three-arched bridge over the River Conwy. It was built in 1636 and is attributed to Inigo Jones though there's no written proof of his involvement. Sometimes known as 'Pont y Perl' (Bridge of the Pearl) it spans a river known since Roman times for its beautiful oyster pearls. At the laying of the foundation stone a pearl was found in the river bed hence the bridge's name.

At one end of the bridge is Tu Hwnt i'r Bont, a restored 15th century court-house now owned by the National Trust and used as a tearoom.

Trefriw

Trefriw nestles below high wooded hills overlooking the Conwy valley and it's here that the river becomes tidal. The village is well situated on the B5106 Betws-y-coed to Conwy road and in summer is well populated with visitors. There are two caravan sites and woodland and riverside walks, but the main attraction for the many coach parties is the woollen-mill. This has been in production for over 150 years and today's visitors can watch the full weaving process and buy goods made on the site. The mill is powered by turbines driven by the River Crafnant, a tributary of the Conwy.

In the hills above the village and reached by a narrow lane, two lakes, Llyn Crafnant and Llyn Geirionnydd, attract many walkers and picnickers. From here several other lakes and pools can be reached either on foot or by car.

Beside the main road to the north of Trefriw is the restored spa whose mineral-rich waters were first discovered by the Romans. Visitors are welcome here and can see the Roman cave and an 18th century stone bath-house complete with slate bath. Displays explain the spa's long history. Until 1939 many of those who came to the spa arrived by paddle steamer from Llandudno and Colwyn Bay.

Afon Crafnant near the Trefriw woollen-mill

Trefriw Walk

All level walking with a muddy track from Llanrwst. 2-2¼ hours.

Parking is available in Trefriw opposite the woollen-mill. Follow the footpath sign down beside the toilet block and follow the narrow path alongside the River Crafnant. Ignoring the footbridge over the river,

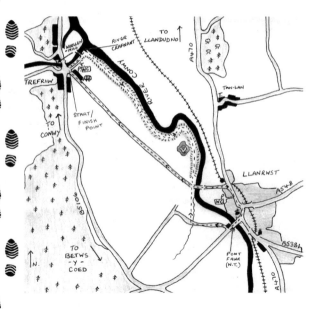

continue along the path, then cross the stile and walk along the embankment. Bear right and follow the embankment; the River Conwy is now on your left. Keeping to the river, continue along the embankment, crossing several stiles until you reach the suspension bridge over the Conwy. Cross the bridge and walk down the lane, then turn right to reach the main road. Turn right again and follow this road through Llanrwst. Continue to bear right (A470) until you reach the B5106 to Trefriw. Turn right over Pont Fawr and walk past the teashop then go down the first track on your right. Continue until you see a ladder stile on your right. Go over the stile into the field and then straight ahead following the hedge. Cross another stile in the corner of the field and continue in the same direction crossing two more stiles before following a small stream on your right. Go through a gap in the hedge then bear right and cross the stile onto the embankment. On reaching the suspension bridge, go left and follow the lane back to the car-park at Trefriw.

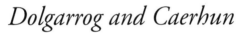

Dolgarrog and Caerhun

Overlooking the reed-fringed, tidal Conwy is the Dolgarrog Hydro-Electric Power Station. The site was originally developed by the Aluminium Corporation in 1907 for their smelting works. In the hills above the Conwy valley, Llyn Eigiau, Coedty Reservoir and the Cowlyd Reservoir provide water for the station by means of a series of tunnels and pipelines.

On the 2nd November 1925, Eigiau dam was breached and the water surged into the Coedty Reservoir which had been full almost to capacity. This overflowed, and water broke through the core wall and cascaded down the hillside into Dolgarrog village. Sixteen people lost their lives in the disaster.

The medieval church at Caerhun near the tidal Conwy

The woodland above and along the hillside to the south of the power station is the Coed Dolgarrog National Nature Reserve. There are some public footpaths skirting the reserve and following the valley of the Afon Ddu but for further exploration of these woods you must apply for a permit from the Countryside Council for Wales office (Ffordd Penrhos, Bangor, Gwynedd). The woodland is rich in flora being less acid than many others in Snowdonia. As well as the pedunculate and sessile oaks there are some marvellous specimens of beech, elm and sycamore.

Two miles north of Dolgarrog near the banks of the River Conwy is Caerhun where a medieval church stands on the site of the Roman fort of Canovium. Traces of the fort can be seen in the rectangle bank surrounding the churchyard.

Ro-wen and the Roman road

The neat and pretty cottages and gardens of Ro-wen give way suddenly to the open, rock-strewn moorland which continues for several miles without a break to the north-west coast and the towns of Penmaen-mawr and Llanfairfechan.

Signs of human habitation going back to prehistoric times can be seen on these mountains high above the Conwy valley. Two prominent standing stones give their name to a pass which can be followed from near Ro-wen to a tarmac lane above the village of Aber, south-west of Llanfairfechan. Bwlch y Ddeufaen (Pass of the Two Stones) is also a Roman road, a wonderful green track which, if followed, gives walkers the opportunity

Countryside near the village of Ro-wen

to explore other ancient remains including the burial chamber known as Maen y Bardd which is near the track about 1 mile west of Ro-wen.

Many ruined cottages and farmsteads can also be seen about the hillside and, a little to the north of

Ro-wen, the deserted church of Llangelynnin proves that there was once a thriving community living on these hills.

There are many public rights of way criss-crossing the moorlands, some easy to follow, others not so easy. The usual caution should be applied when walking on these hills; mists and low cloud can appear suddenly and obliterate any landmarks that you may have been relying on. If you intend venturing away from any of the well-worn tracks, a compass (and the ability to read it) is essential. Although unsightly, and certainly out of place in this ancient landscape, the massive pylons which stride up the mountainside from Dolgarrog and continue to Bangor can provide a useful landmark in case of difficulty.

Ro-wen Walk

A couple of steep climbs; some of the tracks may be muddy or wet and slippery. Allow 2½ hours.

Park in the village car-park. Go back onto the main road and turn right. Before reaching the village centre follow the footpath sign on your left next to the Huw T.Edwards Memorial. Cross the footbridge over Afon Ro then go straight down the path past the cottage and through a metal gate. Now follow this stony track and continue straight ahead until you reach some farm buildings. Bear right and continue along the track as far as the ladder stile. Cross the stile and head straight across the field. Cross another ladder stile, then turn right and follow the hedge all the way round the field until you reach the top left-hand corner. Go through a metal gate and down a muddy, sunken track. Go down on to a farm lane between buildings, turn right along the track, then left across a bridge over the river. Go up on to a tarmac lane, turn left and follow this narrow, steep lane for about 1 mile. Opposite the track to Hafoty-gwyn, turn right onto moorland and walk straight across towards the cottage on the hillside. Go around the cottage and on to a track; follow this until you reach the Roman Road – here a green lane. Turn right past Maen y Bardd burial chamber and follow this track downhill towards Ro-wen. Continue down past the Youth Hostel then, on reaching the houses of Ro-wen, ignore the first lane on your left and continue to the next junction. Turn left and follow this road through the village and back to the car-park.

Tal-y-cafn

Beside the east bank of the river Conwy is the little hamlet of Tal-y-cafn. The Romans would almost certainly have crossed the river near their fort at Caerhun but, in post Roman times, until a bridge was

Tal-y-cafn village

built in 1897, passengers were ferried across the Conwy at Tal-y-cafn. It was considered easier and safer to cross here than near the river's mouth at Conwy. Here is the only bridge for vehicles between the town and Llanrwst. The idea was for travellers to cross the Conwy here and then use the Roman road through Bwlch y Ddeufaen and on to the coastal towns such as Bangor. In 1777 plans were put forward for a proper road to be constructed on the route of Bwlch y Ddeufaen and up until 1811 this road was still being seriously considered for development. The north coast route was deemed unsuitable and too dangerous for the mail coaches. However, when Thomas Telford put forward his plans for a bridge across the river at Conwy, which was eventually built in 1826, the plans for the

Bwlch y Ddeufaen road were scrapped – hopefully for ever.

Today Tal-y-cafn consists of a few houses, an inn, a hotel, and a station on the railway line from Betws-y-coed to Llandudno.

The wooded hills above the village are dotted with several pools and little lakes, the most accessible being Llyn Syberi, south of Tal-y-cafn, and reached from the minor road which leaves the A470 in the village centre.

Bodnant Gardens

Bodnant Gardens, owned by the National Trust, are renowned throughout the world. They were originally laid out in 1874 but it was not until 1949 that they were given to the Trust by Lord Aberconwy. Besides the wonderful flora, the views across the Conwy valley and towards Snowdon are alone worth a visit to the gardens. The gardens are open throughout the year and there is always plenty to see: both native and exotic varieties of flowers, trees and shrubs.

Part of the formal, lawned areas around the house at Bodnant Gardens

The upper part of the garden is the formal area around the house. This consists of lawns, herbaceous borders and some large specimen trees. In the valley of the River Hiraethlyn (a tributary of the Conwy) is the part of the garden known as the Dell. This less formal area contains shade-loving plants, a wild garden and the pinetum.

First to provide colour in the early part of the year are daffodils and other spring bulbs, whilst later on comes a magnificent display of rhododendrons, magnolias and camellias. In the early summer the famous laburnum arch is at its best and the many azaleas provide another blaze of colour.

A favourite time for many visitors is the autumn, when early mists clear to reveal stunning views. In the gardens themselves, shrubs are adorned with brightly coloured berries, and many trees, including the acers, display their splendid colours.

Near the car-park there's a café and lavatories and near the garden entrance, a shop sells plants, garden sundries and gifts.

Conwy

Much of Conwy is still contained within the town walls built, along with the magnificent castle, by Edward I in the latter part of the 13th century. The walls have 21 semicircular towers and the whole project was designed by James of St George – Master of the King's Works in Wales. It was during the Civil War that the castle was last used in military conflict. In 1646, after a three month siege, the castle was taken over by

Cromwell's forces. A visitors' centre describes the history of the castle and town. Those with a head for heights can climb up into one of the turrets giving breathtaking views across the Conwy estuary and beyond.

Conwy quay

In the town, St Mary's church dates from the 14th century and is on the site of the 12th century Aberconwy Abbey. The timber and stone Aberconwy House is early 14th century and is now owned by the National Trust. It houses their shop and an exhibition tracing the town's history from Roman times.

Conwy quay bustles with activity and large crowds gather to watch the fishing boats arrive and land their catch.

Crossing the mouth of the Conwy are three very different bridges, the oldest of which is Telford's suspension bridge, now under the guardianship of the National Trust. The modern road-bridge was built in 1958. Robert Stephenson's tubular railway bridge was completed in the middle of the 19th century.

Glanconwy and Deganwy

A mile and half north of Bodnant Gardens and beside the A470 is Felin Isaf water-mill. Open to visitors, a mill trail provides an insight into the workings and history of water-powered mills.

Near Llansanffraid Glan Gonwy, the RSPB have created a new reserve in an area used to deposit the spoils from the construction of the Conwy tunnel which now carries the A55 expressway under the estuary. Pools have been excavated, hides built and trees planted. Walkways around the reserve ensure that visitors have the opportunity to watch at fairly close quarters some of the thousands of birds that overwinter or breed on the Conwy estuary.

Deganwy station beside the estuary of the Conwy

Beyond the modern bustle and traffic of Llandudno Junction, the small town of Deganwy has a little yachting harbour, and the remains of a castle high up on a hillside overlooking the estuary. It is the last halt on the railway before it reaches Llandudno.

The castle was fiercely defended by the Welsh

against the Anglo-Norman forces attempting to drive their way into Gwynedd.

After Henry III had given the castle to his son Edward I in 1256, Llywelyn ap Gruffudd decided that the castle was so important to the English that it could cause problems for the Welsh. So in 1263 he demolished it and today there is not much to be seen.

Public footpaths up to the site give wonderful views over the mouth of the River Conwy and it's easy to see why it was considered such an important strategic site.

Llandudno

Along with many other seaside towns in Britain, Llandudno developed as a resort during Victorian times. Today it is one of Wales's most popular holiday centres with dozens of sea front hotels, guest-houses and self-catering flats, some of which are open throughout the year. The character of Llandudno has been retained in the sea front buildings and the arcades.

In its position behind the Great Orme headland, Llandudno can

Llandudno pier built in 1877

boast two fine beaches. On the north shore, traditional attractions including pony rides and Punch and Judy shows draw crowds of children and there's safe bathing here too. The west shore, being less sheltered than the north shore, is popular with yachtsmen and windsurfers. Around the town, outdoor activities include golf, tennis, pony-trekking, sailing and fishing.

In bad weather there is still plenty to do in the huge Aberconwy Centre where sports available include badminton and squash. There is also a heated swimming pool. In the Centre, the Arcadia Theatre is the venue for summer shows which attract some of Britain's best loved entertainers.

Alice Pleasance Liddell, immortalised in Lewis Carroll's 'Alice' books, came on holiday to Llandudno during her childhood and an exhibition at The Rabbit Hole in Trinity Square features characters from the books.

The Mostyn Art Gallery in Vaughan Street presents exhibitions showing the depth and variety of Welsh culture.

The Great Orme

The Great Orme's Head is one of the North Wales coast's most prominent landmarks. It rises nearly 680 feet (270 metres) out of the sea and much of it is now a country park.

Prehistoric man made his home here and the 6th century saint, Tudno, established a church when he brought Christianity to the area. Llandudno is named after him. The restored 12th century church is probably on the site of the original building.

The Great Orme visitors' centre has displays showing the history and natural history of this limestone headland. There are many public rights of way up to the summit, some of which are steep and rocky, but the views from the top make the effort worth while. Two easier ways to reach the summit are by cable-car or tram, both of which run frequently during the summer.

The Great Orme's Head

During the Bronze Age, copper was first mined here and the mines are now open to the public. They can best be reached from the tramway or, of course, on foot.

Near the cabin lift terminal, Happy Valley Gardens provide a shady place to sit and rest away from the hustle and bustle of Llandudno. These mainly formal gardens contain exotic as well as native species of flora.

Behind the gardens is Ski Llandudno with its dry ski and toboggan slopes complete with mechanised lifts.

Happy Valley/Great Orme Walk

A very steep climb from the Happy Valley gardens but
generally quite an easy walk; allow up to 2 hours.
 Coming through Llandudno, follow signs for the
Great Orme Scenic Drive. Park in the car-park just past
the pier entrance and before reaching the toll-booth.

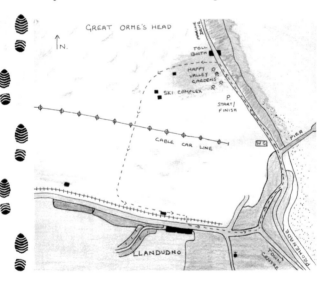

Walk on towards the Great Orme. Just before the
toll-booth, turn left into Happy Valley Gardens. Walk
uphill through the gardens keeping close to the edge
nearest the Great Orme. Continue until you reach the
top right-hand corner next to a shelter. Go through a

wooden gate and walk up the path passing the ski
complex on your left. Climb some steps, then bear left
at the top above the ski tow. Follow the general line of
telegraph poles above the complex, then continue to
follow the grass path towards the cable car line. Go
under the line, walk down the gravel path, then bear left
and follow a grassy path. Before going through the gate,
turn left and follow the fence until you reach a wicket
gate. Go through the gate and continue downhill above
the road and tramway. Now go over the tramway
(taking care to watch for trams from both directions) on
to the road and walk down to the traffic lights.
Continue straight ahead to the next road junction, go
left and follow the road back to the sea front near the
pier. Bear left and continue to car-park.

River
DEE

Introduction

Wales is a land of many rivers, and one of the best known and loved, especially by fishermen, is the Dee.

Its source is in the peaty, rocky lands below the black cliffs of the Dduallt and it is the longest river to originate in the Snowdonia National Park. Above Bala Lake (Llyn Tegid) the river is known as Dyfrdwy and this is its Welsh name along its course.

It soon reaches forestry plantations as it flows in a north-easterly direction towards the lake. At Pont Rhyd Sarn south of Llanuwchllyn it ceases to be a mountain stream and becomes a fast-flowing river.

At the northern end of the lake, Bala is the main tourist centre for the south-east of the National Park. It has good road connections with Dolgellau to the south-west, Llangollen to the north-east and the north coast resorts.

Beyond Bala the Dee continues in a north-easterly direction to Corwen then turns sharply to flow east to Llangollen. Close to the south bank is the busy A5, but for a quieter drive you can follow narrow and sometimes steep lanes to the north of the river. For a few miles between Llangollen and Newbridge another waterway keeps company with the Dee. This is the Llangollen Canal, a branch of the Shropshire Union Canal.

Beyond Llangollen the river Dee leaves behind the mountains of Wales and sweeps through a wide flat valley all the way to its estuary north of Chester. From a point south of Wrexham the river crosses and recrosses the present day border between Wales and England.

OS maps covering the river Dee area are 125, 117 in the Landranger 1:50,000 series and 18 in the Outdoor Leisure 1:25,000 series.

Source and upper reaches

About six miles south-west of Bala Lake the black volcanic rocks of the Dduallt (black hillside) rise to over 2,000 feet (650 metres) between two blocks of commercial forestry. Below these cliffs, Afon Dyfrdwy – soon to become the River Dee – has its source. Many other rivers and streams also have their source in these hills; one of the better known is the Mawddach, which flows in a south-westerly direction to reach the sea at Barmouth.

Experienced walkers may like to tackle the Dduallt but a compass is essential: once out of the forestry there is no proper track across the mountain. It can be approached from Rhyd-y-main on the A494, south of Llanuwchllyn, or from near Dolhendre, north of Bala Lake in the Lliw valley. From the summit there are fine views of the Berwyn Hills to the east and Cader Idris to the south-west.

Upper reaches of river Dee near Pont Rhyd Sarn

There are many other, easier walks in the area although some are not very well waymarked. Remember also that the Forestry Commission allows walkers into their forests unless signs advise otherwise.

The A494 from Dolgellau crosses the river Dee at Pont Rhyd Sarn and nearby there is a camping and caravan site. Most of the other accommodation around here consists of farmhouse bed and breakfast – some available all year.

Llanuwchllyn

Llanuwchllyn lies close to the southern end of Bala Lake, not on the Dee but on the River Twrch, which flows down beside the road from Bwlch y Groes.

North of the village another river, the Lliw, joins in. Near Dolhendre, beside the river, a prominent little hill is marked on maps as Castell Carndochan – a name suggesting a long history of occupation. A castle (possibly 14th century)

Llanuwchllyn church

may have been built on the site of a Bronze Age cairn. It is a ruin today but is a good viewing point. In the 19th century, gold was discovered here, but whether it was for the first time, we don't know. Romans surely passed this way between their fort at Caer Gai north of Llanuwchllyn and their kilns 10 miles to the west beside Sarn Helen – Wales's famous Roman Road. It is quite likely that they knew of the gold and mined it. Today, spoil heaps of crushed white quartz are evidence of the gold mining activities.

In the 19th and 20th centuries, two sons of Llanuwchllyn were foremost in ensuring the survival of the Welsh language.

Owen Edwards was a historian and scholar who wrote many children's books and promoted the use of Welsh in schools. His son, Ifan, founded a Welsh institution that is still going strong today – Urdd Gobaith Cymru (the Welsh League of Youth).

The railway from Dolgellau used to pass through Llanuwchllyn, but the only station here today is the terminus of the Bala Lake Railway.

Bala Lake Railway

The Bala Lake Railway follows the eastern bank of the lake for 4 miles from Llanuwchllyn to Bala. The one way trip takes 25 minutes and you can break your journey at any of the stations along the line for picnicking, sailing, fishing or walking. The line is part of the old Barmouth to Ruabon railway, closed along with many others in the 1960s. The engine used on the line once worked the slate quarries of North Wales. In Britain, North Wales has the highest concentration of privately run steam railways, many running along old industrial lines, but now serving the summer tourist industry.

The only village on the Bala Lake Railway between Llanuwchllyn and Bala town is Llangower. In the churchyard there, the oldest graves are grouped on a low mound that could have been a Bronze Age tumulus.

There are many footpaths up into the hills from the lake. All the lanes seem to end in hilltop farmyards but there are numerous public rights of way worth exploring.

The range of hills to the east of the lake is the Berwyn. Foel y Geifr is one of several peaks at 2000 feet (626 metres) in this south-western edge of the range. The hills are beautiful and covered in heather, but because of this, walking can be difficult except on the most popular paths.

Glyn Gower and Cwm Hirnant, with their mountain streams, provide comfortable and enjoyable walking though the climb up from the lake is quite steep.

Bala Lake railway near Llangower

Near Parc, to the north of the A494 Bala/ Llanuwchllyn road, is Cyffdy Farm where visitors can see all kinds of farm equipment, help feed the farm animals, and enjoy teas and other refreshments.

Llangower Walk

This is a fairly short walk starting off with a steep climb giving a marvellous view over Bala Lake and beyond. It should take about 1½ hours.

Park in the car-park by Llangower railway station.

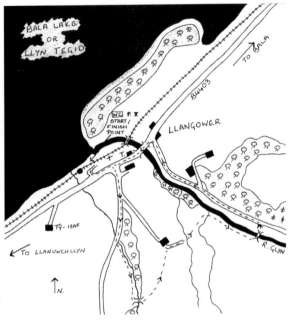

Go out of the main entrance and turn left. Walk
through the village then take the lane on the right,
opposite the church. Walk up this narrow lane (which is
just a farm road), then after the place where a stream
passes under the lane go left through a metal gate; there
should be a footpath sign here.

Walk up beside the stream, go through a gap in the
fence, then turn left and cross the footbridge over the
stream. Follow the path up through the wood and into
the field. Continue straight ahead across the field along
the line of an old hedge. Go over the stile, then down
through the field keeping the farm on your left. Go as
far as the fence, turn right along a track that crosses a

small stream, then go through a metal gate on your left. Walk straight down the field towards the river. Turn right and walk beside the river bank. When you come to the woodland bear slightly uphill onto a track, and then continue until you reach a small wooden gate. Go through the gate, over the footbridge, and across the field onto the lane. Turn left and follow this lane back to the B4403 east of Llangower. Turn left and walk back to the station car-park.

Bala Lake and town

Bala Lake or Llyn Tegid lies in a natural fault between the Aran Mountains to the south and the Arennig Mountains to the north. At 4 miles long it is the largest natural lake in Wales. From the north-east end near Bala the view up the lake is of Aran Benllyn on the left (often topped with clouds), and in the far distance, Cader Idris.

In places the lake is 150 feet (45 metres) deep but the sandy beaches that slope gently down from the railway line provide safe bathing. Fishing and sailing on the lake are controlled by the Snowdonia National Park warden. Information is available from the National Park Centre in Bala. As well as roach, perch and trout there is a more unusual fish that lives in the lake. This is the *gwyniad*—a whitefish of the salmon family found in Britain in Bala Lake only. It is believed to be closely related to the powan of Scotland and the pollan of Ireland. It is notoriously difficult to catch, even with nets, as it lurks right in the deepest parts of the lake. In any case it is now a preserved species.

Bala Lake from the north-east

Bala Lake today is a water sports centre and the river Tryweryn that flows down the eastern side of the town is home to the National White Water Centre and hosts many canoeing competitions.

Bala town consists mainly of one long, wide, tree-lined street. It has a good selection of shops, inns and cafés and there are plenty of guest-houses, hotels and campsites in and around the town. The youth hostel is just east of the town at Rhosygwaliau. Thursday is market day in Bala.

In front of Capel Tegid, on the road to the lake, is a statue of Thomas Charles (1755-1814), a foremost figure in the Methodist revival in North Wales.

Dee Valley near Llandrillo

From Bala the River Dee gains strength as it continues in a north-easterly direction towards Dyffryn Edeirnion. The main A494 is north of the valley whilst the quieter B4402/B4401 follows the river closely, passing through small villages and hamlets overlooked by peaceful, wooded hills.

Prehistoric man left his mark on these hills and in the valley itself. There are three ancient burial sites easily accessible from roads around the Llandrillo area. Beside a minor road and the old railway to the north-west of the village is Branasuchaf. Remains of this Neolithic burial chamber consist of three upright stones and part of the covering mound. About 1½ miles along the same road there is a stone circle near Tŷ Ffos farm. It has fourteen boulders around a slightly raised platform.

Next to the B4401 between Llandrillo and Cynwyd is Rhydyglafes chambered cairn with a large capstone beside a mound. In the surrounding hills there are the remains of many settlements and cairns.

There are several good camping and caravan sites within a couple of miles of Llandrillo. An ancient road (Ffordd Gam Elin) leaves the B4401 about a mile north of the village (the lane next to the telephone box). For a while it is a well-surfaced road but soon deteriorates into a green track. From here there is access on foot to the highest peaks of the Berwyn Hills. The ancient road leads eventually down to Llanrhaeadr-ym-Mochnant.

Llandrillo

Cynwyd

The four-arched bridge over the Dee at Cynwyd is said to be the oldest in the old Merioneth. There are walks on both sides of the river which is reached by taking the road down past the Post Office. The River Trystion comes down from the Berwyn Hills and flows through the village. It is crossed by a solid stone bridge oddly out of proportion to the stream that flows under it.

Cynwyd bridge

If you take the lane opposite the road down to the Dee you can follow the north bank of the Trystion. In about a mile you will come to a small reservoir. Continue then along the lane until it gives way to a forest track, which again peters out. This is another ancient road across the Berwyn Hill – Ffordd Saeson (Englishmen's Road). After crossing the hills the path becomes a track before meeting up with motorable roads, which soon lead over the border to Shropshire. This perhaps accounts for the name of the road.

Just north of Cynwyd a major tributary joins the Dee. This is the River Alwen, which has its source at

Llyn Alwen on Mynydd Hiraethog, south-east of
Llanrwst. It flows into the Alwen reservoir, which is
surrounded by conifer plantations and is neighbour to
another reservoir, Llyn Brenig. Here there are picnic
sites, forest walks and vistors' centres, and at the
northern tip of Llyn Brenig there is an interesting
archaeological trail. The reservoirs and forest are easily
reached by taking the B4501 from Cerrigydrudion, a
village on the A5 about 10 miles west of Corwen.

Cynwyd Walk

Allow 1½ hours; mostly level walking.
   In Cynwyd village park near the Post Office and
then continue down the lane opposite the public house.

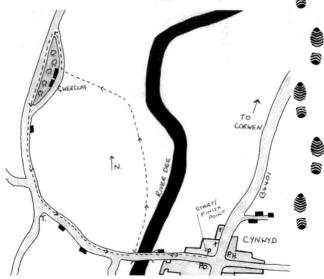

Cross the bridge over the Dee then go down the steps on your right. Walk beside the river, cross the stile and continue beside the river (occasionally the path is some way from the river bank). Bear left away from the river and, near the farm, go over the stile, then turn left up towards the farm buildings. Follow the track round to the right and continue until you reach the lane. Turn left along the lane and, on reaching a phone box, turn left and walk back to the village.

Corwen and Dyffryn Edeirnion

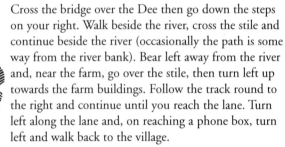

Corwen is an old market town and entrance to the part of the Dee valley called Dyffryn Edeirnion.

Fishing and, of course, hill walking are popular pastimes with visitors to the area. The town is strung out along the A5 and can be a bottle neck for traffic particularly on market day, Tuesday.

One of the most famous establishments in the town is the Owain Glyn Dŵr Hotel, for this central part of the Dee valley is the heart of Owain Glyn Dŵr country.

Owain was Wales's last native Prince, who led an uprising against English rule in the early 15th century. He took his name from Glyndyfrdwy, a village four and a half miles east of Corwen. His real name was Owain ap Gruffudd Fychan and he also had a country seat at Sycharth farther south in the Tanat Valley (Dyffryn Tanad). Owain Glyn Dŵr Mount near Carrog could be the site of his fortified manor.

Owain was descended from the Princes of Deheubarth in South Wales (castle at Dinefwr) and Powys. He studied law in London at the Inns of Court and became a squire to the Earl of Arundel, the Marcher Lord who owned Dinas Brân near Llangollen.

Stone 'fence' beside River Dee at Corwen

Caer Drewyn between Corwen and Carrog is a treeless hill with the fragmented remains of an Iron Age fort. The camp slopes downhill and may have been added to in the Dark Ages. Seek permission to go up to the site and you will be rewarded with marvellous panoramic views.

Carrog is a small village on the north bank of the Dee, three miles east of Corwen. Its fine, five-arched bridge has the date 1661 carved on it.

Corwen Walk

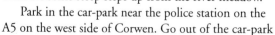

A well-used walk beside the River Dee; allow about 1½ hours. Although level walking beside the river, there are some steep steps up from the river meadow.

Park in the car-park near the police station on the A5 on the west side of Corwen. Go out of the car-park

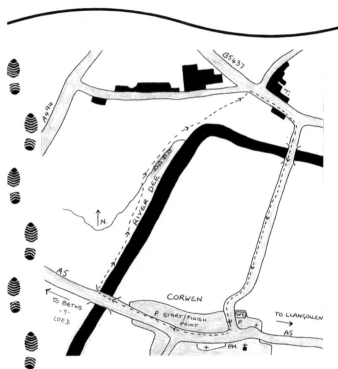

and turn right. Follow the main road around and cross the bridge over the Dee. Go over the stile on your right and walk down beside the river. Continue along the river bank until you reach a line of trees. Bear left and, keeping parallel to the river, walk between the trees and the fence. Cross the stile on the left and follow the fence, then cross a stile on you right into an area of scrub. Follow the worn path, then bear left, cross the stream (stone bridge) and turn right to walk along the path through the bracken alongside a stream. Now, veering away from the stream, climb the steps, go over the stile and then turn right and follow the hedge. Continue along the line of the hedge, go uphill under a large oak tree and a line of pylons, then cross the stile next to the gate. Turn right down the road, take the first turning on the right and walk back to Corwen. In town turn right again and walk back to the car-park.

Llangollen

Llangollen is a town that has grown up around its 14th century bridge. The bridge is traditionally one of the 'Seven Wonders of Wales'.

The parish church is dedicated to the Celtic saint, Collen, and stands above the river just downstream from the bridge. Much of what can be seen today dates from the 14th century.

To discover Llangollen, take a Town Trail Walk (visit the Tourist Information Centre for details). Much of the architecture dates from the 17th and 18th centuries and there are some good examples of Victorian and Georgian town houses. A number of the houses and cottages are in the black and white timbered style reminiscent of nearby Shropshire. The most famous half-timbered house in Llangollen is the

Llangollen bridge

Tudor style Plas Newydd. It was home, in the 18th century, to the two legendary 'Ladies of Llangollen'. These two unmarried Irish ladies, Lady Eleanor Butler and Miss Sarah Ponsonby, had run away from Waterford, and spent their days entertaining such dignitaries as the Duke of Wellington and Sir Walter Scott. The house is open to the public and contains a collection of medieval carvings. The house is surrounded by formal gardens.

In the first week of July, Llangollen plays host to the International Eisteddfod. Every year this festival attracts thousands of visitors from around the world who either take part in the many and varied competitions or just come to watch the colourful spectacle of the performers, many in national costume.

In Wales, Eisteddfodau take place on a national, regional and local basis – even schools and villages hold their own events. The competitions range from singing and dancing to poetry and recitation.

Around Llangollen

Standing high above the town of Llangollen are the ruins of Castell Dinas Brân. This 12th century fortress can be reached by following a path up from the canal near the museum. It's a steep climb up to the ruins but the views from the top are magnificent. The castle was built by the Princes of Powys as a borderland base.

About two miles from Llangollen on the A542 to Rhuthun (and before reaching the famous Horseshoe Pass) are the remains of Valle Crucis Abbey. The name means 'valley of the cross' and the Abbey is tucked neatly below high hills in meadows near the River Eglwyseg.

It was founded in the early 13th century by Madog ap Gruffudd, Prince of Powys, and is one of Wales's Cistercian houses. It is the burial place of the poet Iolo Goch. George Borrow, during his journey through Wales, made a special pilgrimage to see the poet's grave. Unfortunately, when he reached the Abbey and asked the whereabouts of

Valle Crucis Abbey

the grave, nobody seemed to know about it. The Abbey is open to the public and right beside it is a camping and caravan site.

A little farther along the same road is an interesting wayside cross. At least it used to be a cross, though now it is little more than a stone stump surrounded by railings. This is Eliseg's Pillar, named after another Prince of Powys. It is believed to date from the 9th century and originally bore an inscription tracing Eliseg's ancestry through the British High King Vortigern back to Roman times and the Emperor Magnus Maximus.

Thomas Telford and the Llangollen Canal

Pontcysylltau aqueduct

Thomas Telford was born in 1757 in Dumfriesshire, Scotland, the son of a shepherd. He became a stonemason's apprentice in London in 1782 and then, after studying architectural engineering, he was appointed Surveyor of Public Works in Shropshire. Telford worked on road design and building in the Scottish Highlands, but one of his greatest works is the Pontcysylltau aqueduct east of Llangollen.

At the beginning of the 19th century, canals were growing in popularity with the increase in industry, and Telford was commissioned to construct a canal to link the rivers Dee, Mersey and Severn. The Shropshire Union Canal needed to be conveyed across the Dee valley and so work was begun on the Pontcysylltau aqueduct. It was constructed as a trough of cast iron plates carried on a support of nineteen slender stone pillars. It is over 1000 feet (307 metres) long and 121 feet (39 metres) high and, when it was first built, people doubted it could support the weight of water let alone canal traffic. It took ten years to build and cost £47,018. All of it is Telford's original work except for the railings that have since been replaced. The opening ceremony was attended by an estimated eight thousand people.

Telford's other achievements in Wales include the road from Shrewsbury to Holyhead—today's A5— that was the equivalent of a motorway when it was first built. Some of the original toll-houses remain today, a good example being Tŷ Isaf near Llangollen.

Tŷ Mawr Country Park and the Cefn Viaduct

Beside the river Dee and well hidden from the chemical works of nearby Cefn Mawr and the industrial Acre-fair is Tŷ Mawr Country Park. Tŷ Mawr means large house and originally the land was part of a farmstead. Today the thirty-five acres of grassland are home to a range of domestic animals including goats, ponies, hens, ducks, and unusual breeds of sheep. All the animals are child-friendly and the park provides an enjoyable outing for the family especially if combined with one of the many events that take place throughout the year. These range from spinning afternoons for families to egg decorating and wild-flower planting. Rangers lead walks around the park pointing out the most interesting features. Besides farm animals, the woodlands, river and meadows are full of wildlife. You may well see woodpeckers and nut-hatches in the woods, dippers and grey wagtails down by the river and butterflies and bees during the summer in the unspoilt meadows.

At Tŷ Mawr, an old barn has been converted into a visitors' centre and there is also a shop and toilets. On the east side of the park is the stone-built Cefn viaduct carrying the Chester to Shrewsbury railway (nearest station Ruabon). Henry Robertson's design was constructed in 1848 and stands over 150 feet (45 metres) above the river. It took just two years to build at a cost of £72,346.

Just south of Froncysylltau is Pisgah Quarry, a small reserve of the North Wales Wildlife Trust. It was last worked in 1830 and has been colonised by trees, scrub and grasses. It is rich in lime-loving species such as burnet saxifrage, cowslip, field scabious and salad burnet.

Cefn viaduct near Tŷ Mawr Country Park

Tŷ Mawr Walk

A 2 hour walk along the River Dee with a steep climb up to the Llangollen canal with views of the Newbridge viaduct. Part of the walk crosses the 121

foot (39 metres) high Pontcysylltau aqueduct.

Park in the car-park of the Tŷ Mawr Country Park. Walk back towards the main entrance and turn right down a signposted footpath. Take the first footpath on

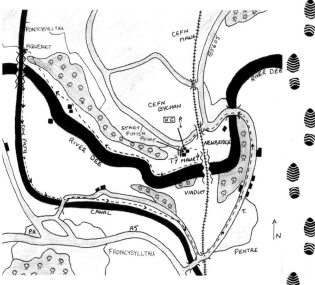

the right, go down through a field, and follow the hedgerow to a stile in the corner of a field. Go over the stile, turn right, and walk beside the river. Now, bear slightly away from the river onto the path and continue parallel to the river until you reach a signpost to 'Aqueduct'. Turn left on to the boardwalk, then bear right and follow the well-worn path, which is now a little way from the river bank. Cross the stile; the aqueduct should now be in sight. Bear right onto a track towards waterworks, then keeping the works on your left, walk through woodland until you are almost underneath the aqueduct. Go right, and mount the steep steps onto the canal towpath. Turn left, walk over the aqueduct, and then continue along the towpath (in places a track or lane) until you reach the main road. Turn left, and follow this road back as far as the railway bridge. Following the signs to the country park, go down a minor road under the railway, and make your way back to the Country Park.

Overton and District

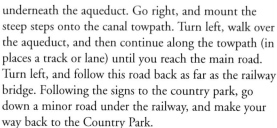

St Mary's church at Overton stands in a circle of yew trees – another of the 'Seven Wonders of Wales' in the rhyme learned by children all over Wales:

> 'Pistyll Rhaeadr, Wrexham Steeple,
> Snowdon's Mountain without its people,
> Overton Yew Trees, Gresford Bells,
> Llangollen Bridge and St Winifrede's Wells.'

The red sandstone church, typical of these borderlands, dates partly from the 14th century with later additions. It is believed to have been built on the site of a much earlier wattle-and-daub church probably from the 7th century. The first stone church may have been built in the 12th century but nothing remains of this except some old stone coffin lids and, of course, the yew trees, which may precede this period.

The name Overton means in old English 'a riverbank settlement' and is the part of Wales called English Maelor. When King Offa of Mercia built his dyke in the 8th century these villages were on the English side as was the settlement now known as Wrexham. The half-timbered and mellow pink houses of Overton are so untypical of Wales that you feel as though you are in England. Indeed the border is only a couple of miles away. East of Llangollen you soon leave the hills of Wales behind and head for a very different landscape: a wide, flat, fertile valley where the roads wander back and forth across the border. The countryside and villages have an air of prosperity with parkland and large, grand farmhouses a regular feature.

Nearby Erbistock is renowned as one of the prettiest Deeside villages and is famous for its 13th century inn.

Overton church

Bangor Is-coed

B angor Is-coed or Bangor-on-Dee is known today for its racecourse situated near the River Dee, south of the village.

The Welsh name of the village means 'monastery under the wood'; the village, home of one of the earliest monasteries in Britain, has a long history for it was active and thriving by the 5th century. It is believed that

Bangor Is-coed church

by AD596, the monastery had 2,400 monks. It was also a college of the Celtic church. During the Battle of Chester in AD615 the monastery was destroyed by armies from Northumbria. Some of the monks managed to flee to Bardsey Island off the Llŷn Peninsula, a place of pilgrimage and refuge.

In the 12th century a chronicler described substantial remains of churches and monastic buildings, but there is nothing to see today.

The narrow, five-arched bridge over the Dee dates from the 17th century and, like the nearby church, is built of local sandstone.

Although the village has good road connections with Chester and the towns of north-east Wales and Shropshire, it is bypassed by the A525 and therefore missed by a large proportion of the holiday traffic.

For a few miles between Bangor and Holt the River Dee forms the modern boundary of Wales; villages on either side of the border are similar in appearance. The names of the farms and hamlets in these borderlands are a mixture of Welsh and English – Sutton Green, Bowling Bank, Is-y-coed and Maes-gwyn Farm.

Bangor Is-coed Walk

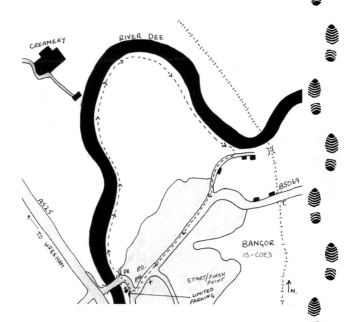

This walk is easy and level and takes about 1½ hours. Park in Bangor Is-coed near the church. Walk towards the old bridge over the Dee, then go past the Royal Oak pub and turn right through the pub car-park. Go down the hard-core track, through a metal gate, then bear left towards the river bank. Continue along a worn path beside the river until you reach some pine trees on an embankment. Cross the stile, and turn right down a lane. At the main road turn right and walk back to Bangor. Bear right and return to the church.

Holt

There are many ancient and lovely bridges over the Dee and one of the best is at Holt, a village right on the English border. Holt looks across the river to the small Cheshire town of Farndon, and the bridge

Holt bridge

separating the two is narrow and dates from the 14th century. There are several riverside walks along both the English and Welsh banks. Walk downstream either side of the river and you will see an unusual feature of these meadows. There are numerous wooden dwellings scattered about the fields, and although most are holiday and summer houses, some are occupied throughout the year.

These meadows are regularly flooded in the winter.

Holt had an Edwardian castle above the river, built of dark red, local stone. The remains can be seen on the east side of the village; near the Post Office, take the footpath that is signposted to the castle gardens.

The 18th century Welsh traveller and scientist Thomas Pennant speculated that the castle was built on the site of a Roman fort. There was a Roman pottery at Holt. Tiles, pipes and other ware have been found in the area.

Holt's church is dedicated to St Chad, a saint from the Dark Ages, and was built about 1400.

Beyond Holt the river Dee continues on a northerly course winding its way to Chester. Within the city the river becomes tidal and has been canalised to control its flow within the low-lying lands between the Wirral and the industrial Connah's Quay on the Welsh side.

Holt Walk

This is a walk that, although quite long, is not strenuous as the walking is mostly level; you should allow 2½-3 hours.

You can park at the picnic site on the Cheshire (Farndon) side of the Dee bridge. Walk back across the bridge and go over the metal rail stile on your right. Go down to the river bank and walk alongside the river. Pass the wooden dwellings on the river bank and continue to the field boundary. Cross the stile onto the farm track and continue straight ahead. When the track peters out, keep walking alongside the hedgerow passing a ruined building on your right. Keep parallel with the river as far as the field boundary, go over the stile, and turn right towards the river bank. Go over the stile, then through rough pasture towards the signs on the river bank. Cross the footbridge over a stream and continue ahead beside the river. Now follow the river, walking along the embankment. Cross three more stiles until the path begins to veer away from the river. Continue to

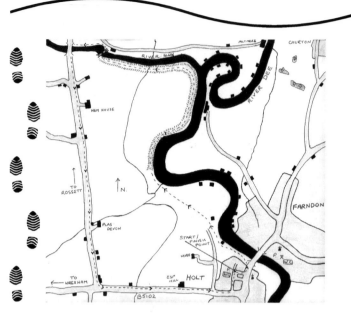

follow the embankment, which now takes you alongside
a minor river and a lane. Walk along to a farm on the
opposite side of the river, cross the footbridge, and go
across to a stile. Turn left and again walk beside the river
until you reach some stone steps, which lead up onto
the main road (B5102). Turn left and follow this road
back to Holt. There is a grassy verge or pavement all the
way, but take care as this is a busy, fast road. In the
village follow signs to Farndon to return to the picnic
site.

Connah's Quay to Holywell

M̲ost of the length of the Dee estuary is very indust-
rialised on the Welsh side but there are still some
interesting towns and villages to explore.

One of the best places
near Connah's Quay is
Wepre Park, a woodland
retreat with a stream, a
golf-course, and the
remains of a hill-fort.
Near the park are the
remains of a 13th century
castle built by Llywelyn
ap Gruffudd.

The busy A548 runs
the length of the Dee
estuary and the next town
on the route is Flint. Flint
officially became a town
when it was granted a
charter by Edward I on
8 September 1284. The
original town walls have

Flint castle

gone and Flint is now a modern, bustling town.
However, Flint does have a wonderfully sited castle –
right down by the estuary behind the railway line. It was
the first of the fortresses to be built by the English King
Edward I. There is a picnic site and parking near the
castle, which is open to the public.

In the past, Flint's prosperity came from iron-ore
mined in the nearby Halkyn Mountain, three miles

inland from the town. The disused workings provide interest for botanists, being rich in many plants favouring spoil heaps, and also for archaeologists interested in Wales's industrial heritage.

The small town of Holywell overlooks the Dee estuary and is named after the curative well of St Winifrede, another of the 'Seven Wonders'.

It has been a place of pilgrimage since the 7th century and is known as the 'Lourdes of Wales'. An ornate chapel was built over the well in the late 15th century.

Mouth of the Dee – Mostyn to Talacre

Religious power in the lower Dee estuary was centred at Basingwerk Abbey near Greenfield, a mile north-east of Holywell. It was founded for the Savignac order in 1132, but within fifteen years had been absorbed by the Cistercians. The substantial ruins are mainly 13th century. The name of the abbey is Saxon, possibly meaning the fortress of a now unknown leader called Basil.

Between Greenfield and Mostyn a public footpath follows the sea wall allowing good views across the estuary. Although it looks Welsh, Mostyn is from the English 'moss' meaning a marsh and 'ton' meaning a settlement. Mostyn Hall to the north-west of the village is a 15th century manor house on the site of a house of the Welsh Princes. Coal and iron were exported from Mostyn quay, which is still used today.

At the mouth of the Dee estuary, Talacre is largely made up of caravan sites mostly deserted in winter.

At Point of Ayr, the Royal Society for the Protection of Birds manages a large reserve consisting of mud-flats with a shingle spit and an area of salt-marshes. It has been designated a Grade 1 Site of Special Scientific Interest for its importance as a feeding and roosting ground for tens of thousands of wildfowl and waders every year.

Point of Ayr

For access to the reserve, turn off the A548 to Talacre and park near the sea wall (just past the Smugglers' Inn). Walk along the sea wall towards the colliery and there is a 'hide' giving good views over the reserve.

In winter look out for large flocks of oyster-catcher, knot, dunlin and ringed and grey plover. In summer, sandwich, common and Arctic terns roost on the reserve. Autumn is a good time to visit the reserve as many seabirds are blown into the Dee estuary by strong winds.

River
DYFI

Introduction

The River Dyfi has its source in the south-east of the
Snowdonia National Park, and for most of its length
can be followed by road or rail. Creiglyn Dyfi is the
source lake of the river and nestles beneath Aran
Fawddwy whose summit is several metres higher than
the better known Cader Idris to the south-west. In the
upper reaches, the river is called Llaethnant – milk
stream – because of its milky appearance as it rushes
towards Llanymawddwy. The countryside around the
Upper Dyfi is characterised by steeply rising hills where
small farms hug the valley floor or are tucked into one
of the many side valleys, sheltered by woodland
wherever this remains. It is a land of soaring buzzards

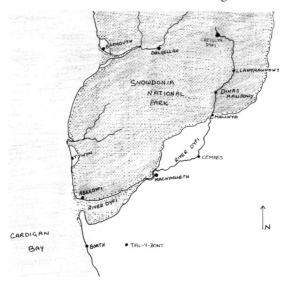

and ravens, grazed by hardy hill sheep and cattle.

Beyond Dinas Mawddwy the valley opens out and good roads now mean access is easy from the rest of Wales. More accommodation becomes available including good country hotels and inns as well as the usual camping and caravan sites and youth hostels. Tracts of commercial forestry clothe some of the hills to the west of the widening valley until the river reaches Machynlleth, the main shopping and tourist centre for the Dyfi valley.

West of Machynlleth, the Dyfi becomes tidal: main roads and the railway follow both north and south banks until the river enters the sea between the holiday resort of Aberdyfi and the dunes of Ynys-las.

OS maps covering the river Dyfi are 135, 125 in Landranger 1:50,000 series and 23 in Outdoor Leisure 1:25,000 series.

Upper Reaches

The twin peaks of Aran Fawddwy and Aran Benllyn are popular with walkers and climbers, and there are several paths up to and along the ridge. The three main routes are from Cwm Cywarch near Dinas Mawddwy, Rhyd-y-main north of Dolgellau, and Llanuwchllyn at the southern end of Bala Lake. None are too difficult, and each ascent is around 2300-2450 feet (700-750 metres), with the summit of Aran Fawddwy at 2970 feet (905 metres).

All these routes begin as public footpaths, but then the walking is along courtesy paths. As the name suggests, these paths are not public rights of

Upper reaches of Dyfi

way but are provided with the agreement and co-operation of walkers and landowners. The availability of these paths to walkers is periodically reviewed by the owners, and taken into consideration are damage to fences and walls, litter and rubbish, and disturbance to farm stock.

There is no path to Creiglyn Dyfi, but it can be seen from the pathway up to Aran Fawddwy. At Blaen-pennant, on the road from Llanymawddwy to Llanuwchllyn, there is a public footpath up to the Dyfi waterfalls. Since they are surrounded by trees they are a much finer sight in winter after heavy rain or a snow melt.

Birds of the Upland River

The uplands of Mid and North Wales are relatively unspoilt by intensive farming, and rivers and riverside meadows can be particularly important for wildlife. Along with woodlands and hedgerows, rivers and river banks provide shelter, food and nesting sites for a wide variety of birds and animals.

Dippers and grey wagtails are typical birds of rocky upland rivers like the Dyfi. The dipper with its distinctive white bib and bobbing action can often be seen sitting on a rock, then suddenly plunging into the river to feed on insects and insect larvae. It literally walks on the bottom of the river and against the flow of the water to catch whatever may be swimming past. They make their domed nests in crevices in the river bank, under bridges or sometimes behind waterfalls.

Grey wagtails also feed on insects around the river bank or they may catch the insects in flight over the river. They are often seen perching on rocks mid stream, flicking their tails continuously. They too will nest in crevices in the river banks.

Although more common in town ponds and lowland rivers, mallard can be found in small groups or pairs in upland rivers and streams.

Alder trees love the dampness of river banks and will tolerate floods; in winter they provide an important source of food for parties of siskins.

Hedgerow trees like hollies and hawthorns provide winter food for berry-loving members of the thrush family including blackbirds, redwings and fieldfares.

Dyfi near Llanymawddwy

Llanymawddwy

From Blaenpennant, the river Dyfi runs parallel with the minor road for about six miles to Dinas Mawddwy. The valley here is still narrow and many streams come tumbling down the hillsides to join the

Inside Llanymawddwy church

Dyfi. One stream that can be explored using public footpaths is the Pumrhyd, which enters the Dyfi near Llanymawddwy. Beside the chapel in the village a signposted path leads up the steep, rocky valley for about 1½ miles to Pistyll Gwyn (White Waterfall). It is more spectacular after heavy rain than the falls on the Dyfi above Blaenpennant.

Another narrow-sided valley is Cwm Pen-y-gelli opposite the Pumrhyd, but there is no public path beside the stream, so if you wish to explore it, ask permission from the landowner. A more unusual feature of this part of the Dyfi valley is patches of rhododendrons whose invasive nature is a problem in some parts of the Snowdonia National Park.

The village of Llanymawddwy consists of a few houses, a chapel, and a church, strung out along the road from Bwlch-y-groes to Dinas Mawddwy. This road is the highest in Wales and at its highest point (1790 feet/546 metres) there is a parking place and wonderful panoramic views.

Llanymawddwy Walk

Park in the village, pulling well off the road if possible. This is quite an easy walk, which follows the river Dyfi and is fairly well waymarked. There are several streams to cross, which could prove tricky in wet conditions. Allow up to 2 hours.

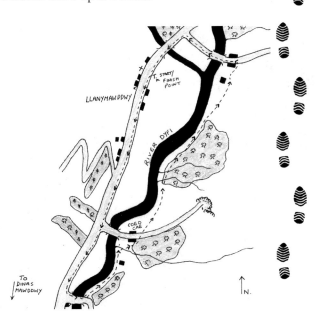

From the village centre walk down the road in the direction of Dinas Mawddwy. Go down the first lane on your left, over the river, then go uphill and take the first turning on your left (track and footpath sign). Walk down a track above the river, then bear slightly towards a wood. At a ruined building, continue ahead, then bear sharp right into the wood, and walk along a grassy track until you find yourself opposite a farm. Bear right following the fence, cross a stream, then go over the stile opposite. Continue straight along a hard-core track, then, just before the gateway, go left downfield, walking beside the fence. Now, you should continue in the same direction, crossing several more stiles and streams until you begin to go downhill near an old ruined farm. Keeping the building on your left, walk down the path through the bracken field, then turn left and walk down to a gateway (there is a post with a yellow dot on it but you may not see it if the bracken is high).

Go through the gateway and down a rocky, muddy track leading to a farm. Go through a gate onto a farm track, then turn left between the farmhouse (on your right) and some farm buildings (on your left). Continue down the farm lane until you reach a junction, turn left again and walk back to Llanymawddwy.

Abercywarch

The hamlet of Abercywarch lies about 1 mile from Dinas Mawddwy where Afon Cywarch joins the Dyfi. The minor road up Cwm Cywarch eventually peters out but several public footpaths lead up into the hills. To the west, the cliffs of Craig Cywarch provide climbers with a challenge and botanists with a rich variety of plant life, which includes the yellow Welsh poppy.

From Blaencywarch near the top of the valley there is access to one of the most popular routes for the ascent of the Aran range. A signposted footpath leads across the Cywarch and continues in a north-easterly direction. At first, the walking is across grassy hillside but it becomes rockier later in the ascent. At a height of 1860 feet (568 metres) there is a

Dyfi at Abercywarch

quartz cairn and here the public path ends. The rest of the ascent across the ridge is along courtesy paths.

At Drysgol (2400 feet/731 metres) the whole Aran range comes into view and you will see the source lake, Creiglyn Dyfi, nestling below Aran Fawddwy.

From here you can follow the whole ridge down to Llanuwchllyn, turn left for Rhyd-y-main, or turn round and follow the same path back to Blaencywarch.

Dinas Mawddwy

In the Middle Ages Dinas Mawddwy was the centre of local power. Today the village is off the A470 road

from Machynlleth to Dolgellau and there is a camping and caravan site, a youth hostel, and inns, hotels and farmhouse bed and breakfast.

In June the patches of rhododendrons make a splash of pink around the village.

The local industries used to be quarrying and mining in the hills surrounding the Upper Dyfi and a short stretch of railway linked Dinas Mawddwy with the main line 7 miles south at

Pont Minllyn

Cemaes Road. It was closed in 1951, and near the old station there is a woollen-mill where visitors can watch the weaving process and buy goods made at the mill.

Nearby, Pont Minllyn is an ancient packhorse bridge over the Dyfi. It is double-arched and covered in grass and moss. It was built by parish rector and scholar, Dr John Davies, in the early 17th century.

Dinas Mawddwy Walk

Allow about 2 hours; mostly level walking except for a fairly steep hill near the start of the walk. The path beside the river may be muddy.

Park in the lay-by on the A470 just north of the garage

and shop at Minllyn. Walk back past the garage and
continue until you see the entrance to Celyn Brithion
caravan and camping site. Turn down into the site and
follow the tarmac road, passing a ruined cottage on your
left and then a white house and farm on the right. The
lane becomes a track. Past the house go through a gate on

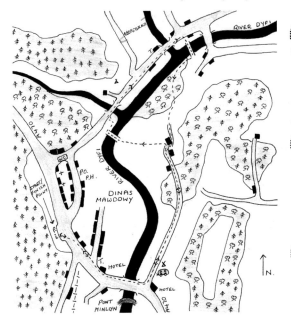

the other side of the road (the footpath is marked by a
yellow dot and post). Walk down the path between some
trees, then go through a wicket gate and over the
footbridge crossing the river Dyfi. Turn right and follow
the bank of the river across the common and onto the
lane. Turn right and follow this lane to the hamlet of
Abercywarch for approximately 1 mile. Go through a

small wooden gate on your right and cross a footbridge over the Dyfi. Turn right and follow the bank of the river, then cross a stile and continue beside the river. At the next stile follow the fence, then bear uphill away from the river along a worn track between some trees. With the wood now on your right, continue through a field, then head for a gap in the hedgerow. Bear left through the hedge and walk along a worn path, keeping the hedge on your right. Go through a gateway and straight on down through the field towards a farm. Soon the path becomes a grassy track and then a hard-core track. Continue down towards the farm. Go through a gate and over a stream, then bear right through another gate and past some farm buildings on to the track. Turn left and walk back through the campsite. At the main road turn right and continue back to the lay-by.

Hill Farming and Forestry

Most of the Dyfi valley is best suited to rearing beef cattle and sheep: except in the river's flood plain, the soil is often thin and the ground steep and rocky.

In summer the animals graze the *ffridd* – sweet upland pasture – but as winter sets in they are brought down to the fields nearer the farm and given additional food to help see them through the sometimes long, cold winter.

Some lambing is done in purpose built sheds, but on some smaller farms the ewes stay outside near the farm and are visited regularly each day around the time they are due to lamb.

Many farms in Wales have the words *hendre* or *hafod* in their names. These recall the days when a shepherd would move with his flock up the mountain in summer and live in the *hafod* – the summer dwelling. *Hendre* was the more permanent winter dwelling of the shepherd and his family.

These uplands of Wales were considered unproductive but found to be ideal for growing commercial forestry – mostly foreign softwoods like sitka spruce, lodgepole pine and Norway spruce (Christmas trees).

Dyfi valley

These plantations have come in for a great deal of criticism over the years for completely changing the landscape of rural Wales. However, at all stages of the forests' growth, there is habitat for a variety of birds and wildlife. There is no doubt that the owners' willingness to allow walkers and picnickers into the forest has opened up large areas of the Welsh countryside.

Since some of the forests have come to maturity and been felled, the replanting that is now taking place takes more regard of the natural features of the landscape. Stream and pond edges are left uncultivated; blocks of trees are planted more in relation to the contours of the hills, and native and semi-native species are included in the replanting programme.

Mallwyd and the Red Robbers

Mallwyd village with Brigands' Inn on right

The small village of Mallwyd stands back from the A470 near its junction with the A458 to Welshpool. The name could have come from *maen llwyd* – grey stones – which would refer to the pointer stones used by travellers.

The well-known Brigands' Inn in the village commemorates a notorious band of robbers and animal rustlers active in the 16th century. They were known as the *gwylliaid cochion*, red robbers, because of their distinctive colouring. It is said that as many as eighty were hanged by order of the Sheriff of Merioneth on Christmas Eve 1554. According to the story they finally disbanded in 1555.

Not so evident now, but certainly commented on by George Borrow and later travellers, was the prevalence of red-haired folk in the farms and villages around the Dinas Mawddwy and Mallwyd area. It is not known exactly where this colouring came from but one explanation is that they may be descendants of Danes or Normans. Another, more plausible theory is that the early occupants of Wales – the Gaels – are the direct ancestors of the natives of Dinas Mawddwy and Mallwyd and, for some reason, their colouring has survived in this small pocket of North Wales. This would, of course, make them cousins of the red-haired people of Scotland and Ireland.

Mallwyd

Mallwyd church stands sheltered from the main road by a row of trees and dates from the 17th century. It has a plank tower with Latin lettering, and above the door are bones from a prehistoric ox probably dug up from a local peat bog. The village mainly consists of a group of stone cottages and is best explored on foot – park in the telephone box lay-by.

Lovers of prehistoric sites will have noticed the absence of early man's influence on these hills surrounding the Upper Dyfi. However, if you take the A485 from the roundabout at Mallwyd,

Doorway to Mallwyd church

you will soon be in hill-fort and tumuli country. One of the best hill-fort viewing points is Moel Ddolwen above the Afon Gam south of the village of Llangadfan. There are public footpaths up to and around the fort.

About 10 miles east of Mallwyd, three rivers meet near Llangadfan. Afon Twrch has its source just outside the National Park boundary east of Llanymawddwy and flows into the Banw, which is also joined by another river from the south, Afon Gam. The countryside around Llangadfan is hilly and partly forested to the north and west. There are many footpaths across the hills and along the river valleys. Some of these rights of way are sections of the long distance path called Glyn Dŵr's Way; leaflets describing the walk are available at local Tourist Information Centres (the nearest one is Machynlleth). North of Llangadfan, the Dyfnant Forest has footpaths and a waymarked forest trail at Parc Llwydiart where there is also a camping and caravan site and a picnic site beside the river Fyrnwy.

River Dyfi and Dyfi Forest

To the west of the river Dyfi, between Mallwyd and Cemaes, are the extensive conifer plantations known as the Dyfi Forest. The forest straddles the southern boundary of the Snowdonia National Park and stretches westward (with some gaps) to Tal-y-llyn, and south to Pennal above the tidal Dyfi. It is intersected by only one main road – the A487 Machynlleth to Dolgellau road – besides a narrow minor road from Corris. This leads you into the heart of the forest but peters out into farm and forest tracks at Aberllefenni. Here there is parking, a picnic place, and a forest trail. One of the best walks from here is up Cwm Ratgoed, and if you are feeling energetic you can continue in a north-westerly direction to the A487, then walk across the hills to Dolgellau or south-west to Cader Idris.

Dyfi near Cemaes

Whilst you are in the area, stop at the village of Corris, which is about 5 miles north of Machynlleth. Here there is an excellent craft centre, a railway museum, and accommodation in a youth hostel and bed and breakfast inns and farmhouses.

Aberangell is a quiet little village on the western bank of the river Dyfi about two miles south of Mallwyd. Here there is a lovely riverside caravan park and yet more forest, moorland and streamside walks.

The River Dyfi is wide here and, except in times of heavy rain and flood, shingle beaches and sandy banks are exposed. There are welcome patches of mature native and semi-native woodland above the valley floor and within the forestry plantations.

As an alternative to the A470 a narrow lane follows the west side of the valley from Dinas Mawddwy to Cemaes Road.

Cemaes

The village of Cemaes was a staging post on the old coaching road between Machynlleth and Mallwyd. The church stands above the river. There are ancient yews in the churchyard and inside, the remains of a carved screen depicting a trail of vine leaves.

The area is popular with fishermen and the old roadside inn is well patronised by locals and visitors alike.

Above the village to the east is Mynydd Cemaes, a long plateau giving good views along the Dyfi valley. Moel Eiddew at 1486 feet (453 metres) is the highest point and is topped by a prehistoric cairn and a modern triangulation pillar. There are many footpaths up the hill and alongside the streams that rush down to join the Dyfi near the village. A very recent addition to this mountain is a group of wind turbines. These new landscape features are set to become a more regular sight throughout upland Wales in the future.

At Cemaes Road a collection of houses stands near the Aberystwyth to Shrewsbury railway and

Cemaes church

the junction of the main roads from Machynlleth to Newtown, Welshpool and Dolgellau. The river that flows into the Dyfi near the village is the Twymyn, which follows the railway from Llanbryn-mair through a lovely valley to Comins-coch.

Cemaes Road to Machynlleth

Just beyond Cemaes Road the B4404 turns north across the Dyfi and this old coaching road continues almost to Machynlleth.

About 1½ miles from the bridge over the Dyfi, Llanwrin is a little village set in beautiful, quiet countryside with a backdrop of wooded hills and overlooking the wide Dyfi valley. The Early English church has ancient stained glass and a very fine rood screen.

To the south of the Dyfi, several lanes lead off the A489 into hilly countryside with interesting little villages and hamlets. Nearly all these lanes peter out but there are many paths, tracks and old drovers' roads that lead across the north of the Plynlimon range.

Llanwrin church

Penegoes is a village on the A489 about 3 miles east of Machynlleth. The landscape artist, Richard Wilson, was born in the rectory in the early 18th century. Near the village there is an ancient bridge called Felin Gerrig (Mill Stones). The road itself is believed to date from Roman times. There are two stories relating to the name of the village. It is traditionally said to mean 'Head of Egoes' – *Pen* means 'head' and Egoes was a Celtic chieftain whose head is said to be buried beneath a grove of oaks near the church. In the 1950s an attempt was made to fell the trees but local protest was so strong that the idea was abandoned. The other explanation for the name is that *egoes* is the plural of *ag* – an 'opening' – and could refer to the village being near the head of five valleys. Beside a stream in the village is Felin Crewi, a restored water mill, where, as well as seeing the milling process, you can enjoy excellent wholemeal refreshments.

Machynlleth

The principal town on the River Dyfi is Machynlleth, a market town given its charter in 1291. Maengwyn Street is wide and accommodates the thriving Wednesday market and has probably done so for the last seven centuries. In the early 15th century the town was chosen by Owain Glyn Dŵr (Wales's last native Prince) as a base for the principality's only independent parliament (so far). The Owain Glyn Dŵr Institute probably stands on the site where the Parliament met.

In Maengwyn Street, interesting buildings include a black and white house dated 1628. There are several

craft shops in the town and a very good Tourist
Information Centre. Plas Machynlleth was built in 1671
and is surrounded by wooded grounds which today are
the town's park. The Plas was given to the town by the
Marquis of Londonderry shortly before the Second
World War and now contains the council offices as well
as art and craft exhibitions.

The clock tower at the town's cross-roads dates from
1873 and is much photographed and admired by lovers
of Victoriana.

The railway station is
just to the north of the
town towards the Dyfi
Bridge. The bridge itself
dates from about 1530
and is on the site of a
much older river crossing.

Just off the A487,
about three miles north
of Machynlleth, is the
Centre for Alternative
Technology sometimes
called the Quarry.
Whether you have two
hours to spare or a
whole day, a visit to the
Centre is a must. As
well as demonstrating
renewable sources of

Machynlleth

energy such as wind, water and solar power, it has a
shop packed with hundreds of 'environmentally
friendly' items and a whole-food restaurant serving
food grown in the organic garden and plots. When it

first opened, it was dismissed as the brainchild of cranks. Today, however, it attracts thousands of visitors by presenting a lifestyle that is increasingly accepted as the most sensible for the future.

Machynlleth Walk

An easy, level walk taking in the town of Machynlleth; allow 2-2½ hours.

On the A489 park on the grass verge just east of the turning to Plas Dolguog Hotel and next to the river Dulas. Alternatively, park in the cemetery car-park on the left-hand side before crossing the bridge. Walk back

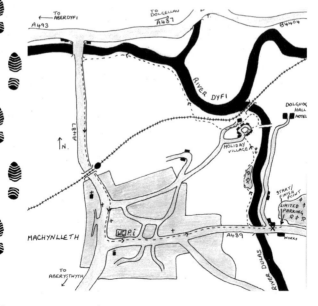

across the bridge and down the steps beside the river. Go over a stile in the corner of a field and continue alongside the river. Just past two houses on the opposite bank, bear left away from the river and walk up through some woodland. Now continue along the river where possible (in places you may have to climb up into the wood, but always keep parallel to the river). After crossing a small stream, climb up a bank into a caravan park, then turn right and follow a tarmac road until you reach a hard-core track on your right that leads back down to the river. Go down to the river, turn left, and continue until you reach a railway bridge over the river. Go left through a field, then through a metal gate onto a lane. Turn right and continue to a sharp corner; just past this corner, go over a stile on your right and through a field along a worn path. Continue alongside the railway and river, then the path will take you downhill towards the railway line. Cross a white stile and go over the railway, taking great care. Once over the railway, turn left and follow the bank of the Dyfi all the way to the bridge. Go over the stile, turn left, and walk back to Machynlleth. Opposite the clock tower turn left onto the A489 and walk back to your vehicle (approximately 1 mile).

The Tidal Dyfi and Cwm Einion

South of Machynlleth the river Dyfi becomes tidal and at the small village of Derwen-las, on the south side of the river, there used to be a thriving port. Its exports were lead and slate and lime was one of its major imports. Today it is hard to believe that any boats could ply their trade from here.

The main-line railway runs parallel to the river and the road and there is a station nearby at Dyfi Junction. The narrow gauge line from Corris used to extend to here until it was replaced by the main line in the 1860s.

Over the river from Derwen-las, the village of Pennal has a long history. The Romans had a fortress here and beside the lane to Plas Talgarth there is a castle motte (mound) probably dating from the 12th century.

Cwm Einion near Furnace

As it is on the main road to Aberdyfi, the village is often traffic-choked, especially the narrow bridge over the Rhonwydd stream that comes rushing down the hills through the Dyfi Forest. For all that, it is a village worth exploring with an interesting little church, a large chapel behind the main road, and a cosy pub, which is crowded in summer with families from the nearby camping and caravan sites and holiday villages.

Back on the south side of the Dyfi and a short distance on from Derwen-las, the Einion stream joins the Dyfi and has a valley that has long been popular with artists and photographers

attracted to its waterfalls and wooded hills. It is called
Artist's Valley on the road signs and can be reached by
road from near the furnace in the village of the same
name (Ffwrnais). From the top of the valley, countless
tracks lead across through forestry to lakes, waterfalls,
and the windswept hillsides of the Plynlimon range.

Ysgubor-y-coed

The parish of Ysgubor-y-coed includes the village of
Eglwys-fach, the estate of Ynys-hir and Furnace beside
the A487. The name means 'barn of the wood' but it is
unclear exactly to what this refers. It could be that it recalls
a medieval tithe barn. The furnace itself dates from 1755
and was built on the site of
much earlier silver mills.
The Einion stream
supplied the power for the
furnace bellows, the height
of the much photographed
waterfall having been
raised to divert the stream
to the mill wheel. Iron ore
was brought here from
Lancashire by sea and
estuary, and the oak woods
of the area – particularly
the Llyfnant and Einion
valleys – supplied the
charcoal. These woods
were considerably depleted
but partially replanted for

The furnace beside A487

timber production and pheasant covers.

Today the furnace is open to the public and information on the history of the area is available at the site. The steep, narrow lane that leaves the A487 north of the furnace ends in a hill farm but from here you can walk for many miles across the Plynlimon hills. The 'little church' of Eglwys-fach dates from the early 19th century with gravestones in the churchyard dating from 1700. The poet R.S.Thomas was vicar at Eglwys-fach from 1954 to 1967.

To the north of Eglwys-fach, Glandyfi Castle is a large Victorian house built on the site of a stone fortress that itself was built to replace a 12th century castle at Domen Las within the RSPB's Ynys-hir reserve. The house is surrounded by wooded grounds and has commanding views over the Dyfi estuary and beyond.

Ynys-hir

In 1965 the owner of the Ynys-hir estate, W.H.Mappin, insisted that after his death the estate should remain a sanctuary for birds. His widow duly sold it to the Royal Society for the Protection of Birds and today it is one of the most popular reserves owned by the Society. To the east of the A487 above Eglwys-fach, the hill called the Foel is part of the reserve and there are several public rights of way across it. The climb is steep but the views are magnificent over the Dyfi estuary and beyond to the southern hills of Snowdonia.

Access to the main part of the reserve is down a lane beside the church in Eglwys-fach. It is well signposted and there is a car-park on the main road near Furnace or you can drive up to the visitors' centre where there is a shop and toilets. From here footpaths lead through woodland, farmland and down to the estuary hides.

Ynys-hir RSPB Reserve

The reserve has such a wide variety of habitats that it provides good bird-watching at any time of year. Many people come in autumn and winter to watch the white-fronted geese, waders and ducks on the estuary. The Marian Mawr pools provide shelter for ducks and can easily be seen from the hide at the edge of the water.

In spring and summer, birds typical of the mixed woodlands of Mid Wales are abundant on the reserve: those to look out for include redstart, garden, wood and willow warblers, spotted and pied flycatchers, all three species of woodpeckers, and several members of the tit family.

Woodland glades and the unspoilt grasslands provide a haven for numerous butterflies and the wetter areas and pools have significant numbers of dragonflies.

Near the Domen Las hide there is a well-established heronry. In early summer the hide is closed to prevent disturbance to the nesting birds.

Pennal Walk

A fairly long walk along and above the Dyfi estuary; allow up to 3 hours.

Park in Pennal, either by the church or the toilet block off the A493. Cross the main road and walk as far as the school. Go through the gate opposite, and walk down a hard-core track beside a stream, then go through a metal gate and cross over the stream. Turn sharp right through a gate and follow the bank of a stream through the field. Cross a ladder stile and continue beside the stream. Cross a footbridge, then, leaving the stream behind, go into the wood. Now keeping the drainage ditch on your right, go straight across the field. Go up an embankment beside the river, turn right and walk along the embankment. Continue until you reach a footbridge over a ditch on your right. Cross the footbridge and head across a field towards a farm (keeping the ditch on your left). Near the farm, turn left through a gate, then through the first gate on your right onto the farm lane. Turn right and follow the lane for approximately ½ mile. Pass a turning to Penmaen-bach and a new bungalow on your left, then cross the first stile in the hedgerow on your right. Go straight up the field, and through a metal gate next to some tennis courts. Bear left then right, up a tarmac lane towards some chalets and a big house. Continue straight ahead to reach a gate into a field.

Go through the gate and walk uphill towards a wood. Inside the wood turn right down a slope and then left to follow a grassy track next to the fence-line. Continue beside the fence (now the wood is on your

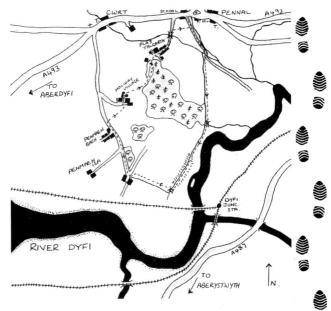

right) until you see a stile on your right. Turn back into the wood, then bear right and follow the path next to a handrail; continue past a hut, then bear left and soon you will reach a tarmac road. Turn left between some holiday homes (Plas Talgarth is on your left) and continue to a junction. At the junction go right and follow this road to a point just after it crosses a stream. Go over a ladder stile on your right, go straight across a field and onto a hard-core track. Turn left and this will take you back to the starting point opposite the school in Pennal.

Aberdyfi

Aberdyfi is a former port on the north side of the Dyfi estuary opposite the dunes of Ynys-las. Cargoes passing through the port included timber, lime, animal hides and wool. The village is conveniently situated on the A493 from Machynlleth to Tywyn and has rail connections with Aberystwyth, Machynlleth and the North Wales resorts.

Aberdyfi

Today the village is a centre for sailing and Outward Bound activities but also attracts visitors hoping for a traditional seaside holiday – with not too much rushing about. There is plenty of car and coach parking in and around the village but in summer it does get very crowded. Weekly car parking tickets can be purchased in the village. There are dozens of hotels, guest-houses and self-catering flats available in the area but you should always book ahead in season. A visit to the National Park information centre on the sea front is a good place to start your holiday with information on places to visit and things to do whatever your interest may be.

Penhelig Park in the village is a good place to go for a sit down amongst the immaculate lawns and flower beds.

Many footpaths lead up into the hills above Aberdyfi; one of the most popular is up to the Bearded Lake in Happy Valley where King Arthur reputedly rode.

A legend connected with Aberdyfi tells of a city sunk under the sea whose bells can be heard ringing in time with the swell of the waves. The story was recorded in the famous song 'The Bells of Aberdyfi' composed by Debden for his opera, *Liberty Hall.*

Aberdyfi Walk

A fairly long walk starting with a steep climb. Allow 2½-3 hours.

Park in the small car-park almost opposite Penhelig station just on the east side of Aberdyfi. Walk back down to the main road, turn right and, just past the toilet block, turn up a track on your right (unsuitable for motors). Go up the track, bear round to the left and go up some steps. Continue up a worn path above the village and round the side of some new houses. Follow this path high above the river estuary until you reach a holiday-homes complex. Bear left, and keeping the houses on your right, walk down a path beside one of the houses and go up some stone steps following a footpath sign. Continue up these steps then, leaving the complex behind, walk straight ahead up a narrow path between bracken and gorse. Bear left following the yellow arrows, then cross a stile and go straight ahead through a field. Now turn right, keeping a gorse-covered hump on your right and following the line of the river estuary. Bear left again around the side of the hill and walk down a well-worn path; cross a stile and continue downhill parallel to a stream. Near the stream, cross a stile on the right, walk beside the stream for a short distance, then go over the stream and cross a ladder stile on the bank. Go up into a field, then bear left and go through a gap in the hedge. Go diagonally across a field towards the old hedge-line, then straight ahead towards a farm. Keeping the farm on your right, go through a gate onto a farm lane. Turn left down the lane and continue until you come to a junction. Turn left again and walk down a lane past a chalet complex until you reach another junction (about ½ mile). Go straight across, down the track, pass a small reservoir and

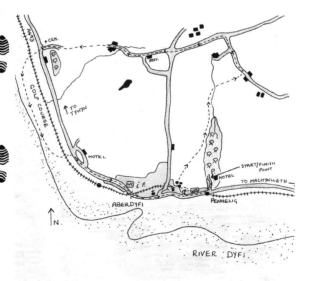

continue. Gradually the track bears right and you now approach a farm. Go through a gate into the farmyard and continue up the track, keeping the farmhouse on your right. Follow this track beside the hedge on your right, then after going through two more gates turn right (there should be a footpath sign) and follow the fence up through the field. Now descend on to an old track and continue until your reach the main road (the track is steep in places and also follows a small stream). On reaching the main road, go across to a lay-by and down a tarmac track to the railway. Cross the railway line and now you are on the golf-course.

Go left and walk back to Aberdyfi (you must follow footpath signs on the golf-course). Cross back over the railway line where there is a ladder stile then, once back on the main road, turn right and walk back to Aberdyfi. Continue through the village to the car-park.

Dyfi National Nature Reserve and Borth

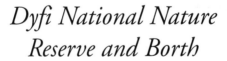

In 1968 the Nature Conservancy Council designated over 2,000 hectares of the Dyfi estuary a National Nature Reserve. It includes the RSPB reserve at Ynys-hir, Cors Fochno (or Borth Bog) and the sand dunes at Ynys-las. It is recognised as being one of the most important estuaries in Britain for wintering wildfowl, has an excellent but threatened dune system and, in Cors Fochno, one of the largest remaining 'raised' bogs in Britain. Because of its sensitive nature and the danger to unwary walkers, there is no public access to the bog but guided walks are sometimes arranged for small groups; details at Ynys-las information centre. A good view of the bog can be had from the public footpath alongside the Afon Leri. The wilderness is generally of most interest to botanists, with its wide variety of plants including sedges, three species of sundews, mosses and, in spring, the bog rosemary with its pale pink bell-like flowers.

Ynys-las, part of of the Dyfi National Nature Reserve

Over Cors Fochno you may be lucky enough to see hen harriers, short-eared owls and merlins. Bordering the west of Cors Fochno, the Afon Leri has been canalised to help prevent flooding.

At the mouth of the Dyfi estuary, Ynys-las dunes are a popular place for families throughout the summer months. Cars can be parked right on the beach and boardwalks lead across the dunes. Throughout the year activities are arranged for children. There are also guided walks and bird-watching sessions led by experts.

Around the small town of Borth there are several caravan sites and, in the town itself, a variety of hotels and guest-houses and a youth hostel. There is a railway station on the main line from Aberystwyth to Machynlleth.

River

River
TEIFI

Introduction

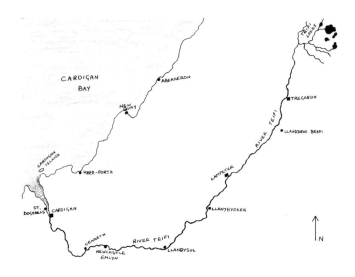

Like the Tywi, the river Teifi has its source in the
southern Cambrian mountains in an area of high,
grassy, undulating country susceptible to low cloud and
sudden mists. By the time it flows under the bridge at
Pontrhydfendigaid it has changed from a mountain
stream to a river hurrying down to the wilderness of
Cors Caron. Once it leaves the bog progress is more
sedate and the valley begins to widen particularly to the
west. Near Cellan on the B4343 the river is right beside
the road and flooding can be a problem.

Between Llanddewibrefi and Llanybydder the
countryside is gentle and pastoral with dairy farms and

little hamlets often dominated by a church or a chapel. Beyond Llanybydder the river enters a series of narrow, rocky gorges, spectacular after heavy rain. The bridges at Maesycrugiau and Henllan provide good viewpoints. The river continues in this mood over the salmon leap at Cenarth, slows a little at Llechryd then becomes tidal at Cilgerran. From here it's less than 10 miles to the sea cliffs at Gwbert where the Teifi flows out into Cardigan Bay.

Today the Teifi valley is popular as a holiday destination in itself – not just somewhere to pass through on the way to the west coast resorts.

None of the towns is a large shopping centre but most are good (and very busy) on market days. OS maps covering the river Teifi are 147, 146 and 145 in the Landranger 1:50,000 series.

Teifi Pools

The source of the river Teifi and the nearby Teifi Pools are in what is regarded as one of the finest stretches of high grassland so far left undisturbed by conifer plantations. The minor road that leaves the B4343 at Ffair-rhos takes you into the heart of this wild lonely country that forms a part of Wales sometimes known as 'The Great Desert'!

There is parking overlooking the largest of the pools, Llyn Teifi. You can also walk down to the dam on Llyn Egnant, the most easterly of the pools. It is a very popular place in good summer weather.

Here the public road ends but you can continue on foot along the track and reach, in less than 3 miles, the head of the Claerwen reservoir, part of the Elan Valley reservoirs scheme.

It is very easy to lose your way up here as each grassy ridge looks very much like its neighbour. If you decide to venture off the main track you should really use a compass to keep your bearings.

You may decide to take the path that bears north-east off the main track and sometimes marked on maps as an 'ancient road'. This leads eventually to the head of the Craig Goch reservoir and was once used by drovers. Part of the way is known as Pedolfa (shoeing place) referring to the drovers' practice of shoeing the animals for their long walk. The pathway was almost certainly used by the monks from Strata Florida on their way to the abbey at Abaty Cwm-hir, a few miles north-east of Rhayader (Rhaeadr Gwy).

Near the Teifi pools

Strata Florida Abbey

In the upper reaches of the river Teifi near the village of Pontrhydfendigaid are the remains of a 12th century Cistercian settlement. In 1164 monks travelled from the abbey at Whitland (Hendy-gwyn), west of Carmarthen (Caerfyrddin), and established a monastery here. In Welsh (Ystrad Fflur) and Latin (Strata Florida*)*, the name of the monastery means flowery levels or flowery vale. Indeed, the nearby meadows, left undisturbed by modern farming methods, are ablaze with wild flowers in spring and summer.

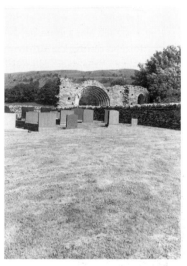

Strata Florida Abbey

The abbey was completed in the 13th century and became an important producer of sheep and lead from the hills nearby. The monks had grazing rights over large tracts of the southern Cambrian Mountains. They also stocked the Teifi Pools with trout and eels. During the 13th century, nine minor Welsh princes were buried at Strata Florida, thus confirming its status. In the 14th century the renowned Welsh poet, Dafydd ap Gwilym, was reputedly buried under the yew tree at the abbey. The most notable surviving feature of the abbey is the distinctive Celtic-Romanesque west door. There is a gift shop and small museum within the Abbey grounds. Pontrhydfendigaid means in English 'the bridge by the blessed ford' referring to the Abbey a mile away.

Tregaron Bog (Cors Caron)

Tregaron Bog covers around 792 hectares and has been designated a National Nature Reserve. A shallow lake formed during the last major glacial period after the valley of the river Teifi was blocked by a terminal moraine at Tregaron. As the lake slowly filled with sediment, open water plants were replaced by reeds whose remains then formed peat. Gradually the area dried out and trees grew, including alder, birch and oak. However, when rainfall increased in the area the trees died out as the water levels rose. Sphagnum mosses thrived and formed acid peat; accumulation of the peat resulted in the three raised bogs, which are the main feature of the reserve.

Beside the old railway line at Cors Caron

Over 40 species of birds breed on the reserve including mallard, teal, curlew, black-headed gulls, and grasshopper and sedge warblers.

Wintering birds include widgeon and whooping swans. Buzzards, red kites and sparrow-hawks are often seen over and around the reserve.

Peat extraction ceased about 20 years ago and

now management of the reserve includes creating shallow pools (flashes) to encourage wildfowl and to help control the invasive scrub.

A public nature trail follows part of the old Carmarthen to Aberystwyth railway for about a mile to an observation tower that gives panoramic views over the reserve. For access to the rest of the footpaths, which take you along boardwalks to the bank of the river Teifi, you must obtain a permit from the warden. The address can be found in information leaflets available along the nature trail.

Tregaron

Tregaron is a little market town with thriving livestock sales attracting buyers and sellers from many miles around. It nestles between high hills to the east and the more fertile River Teifi valley to the west.

In summer the town is a popular stopping-off place for visitors and has a Tourist Information Centre and a very good craft centre.

Tregaron is named after a saint of Irish origin, St Caron, who also gave his name to the nearby Cors Caron (Tregaron Bog). St Caron's church has a 14th century tower and stands on a mound under which the saint is supposed to have been buried. The church was extensively restored in the 19th century.

George Borrow visited Tregaron during his walk through Wales and stayed at the Talbot Hotel. The statue in front of the hotel is that of Henry Richard, born in Tregaron in 1812. He was the MP for Merthyr Tydfil (Merthyr Tudful) and known as the 'Apostle of

Peace' for his work with the Peace Union, forerunner of the United Nations. Another famous son of Tregaron was Twm Siôn Cati, now more often associated with the Upper Tywi valley.

Tregaron

A narrow road running east from the town is the old drovers' road, still a remote drive, but in places it is now deep in the forestry. This joins with the narrow road up the Camddwr valley from Llyn Brianne, or you can continue in an easterly direction across the headwaters of the reservoir and eventually drop down to Abergwesyn.

Llanddewibrefi

Llanddewibrefi lies on the B4343 about 1 mile east of the river Teifi. Over the river, just to the north-west of the village, is the site of the Roman fort of Bremia. Remains found at the site include a legionary stone with a Latin inscription. The village is named after St David, the patron saint of Wales. According to legend, he preached here to such a large crowd that the ground rose beneath his feet in order that he could be heard. This is the mound on which the church stands.

The second part of the village's name also has a legend attached to it. The stream that flows down from the hills beside the church is called Brefi ('you bellow') and some people say that the name refers to the noise the stream makes when it is in flood. However, legend has it that during the building of the church an ox died whilst hauling stones up the slope. One of its companions bellowed nine times and a level track appeared in the hillside.

Today, Llanddewibrefi is quite a large village. It has grown quite considerably in recent years but, with its attractive stone cottages, a traditional Welsh pub, and a large chapel in the village centre, it has managed to retain its Welsh character.

Village centre, Llanddewibrefi

South of the village there are old, interesting bridges over the Teifi at Pont Gogoian and Llanfair Clydogau.

Llanddewibrefi Walk

Allow 2-2½ hours. The walk is mostly through fields and along tracks, with some marshy ground near the river.

Park in the lay-by near the entrance to Tan-'rallt Farm just south of Llanddewibrefi. Walk back towards the village and go up the track to Llwyn Farm. At the farm continue on the hard-core track leaving the farmhouse on your left. When the track peters out, go

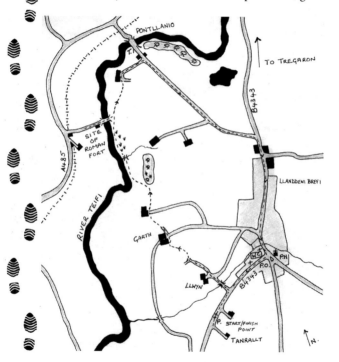

through the gate on your right and follow the left hedgerow through the field. At the next field boundary go straight ahead towards another farm. Cross the stile and go through the double gates. Turn right up the track and then left towards the farmhouse. Through a gate next to the farmhouse you must now follow the hard-core track until again this peters out. Continue straight ahead following the fence across a field towards the next farm. Keeping the farm buildings on your left, go through two gates, cross the farm track and then go through another gate almost opposite. Follow a well-worn track slightly uphill through the field towards a small wood; when the river comes into sight walk down to the bank. Following the river you cross a small stream then a marshy area and you will see a footbridge over the river Teifi. There is a public footpath across the bridge to the site of a Roman fort.

Continue alongside the river until a small fence obstructs the way. Now you must bear right, away from the river and towards the next farm. Keeping the hedgerow on you left, walk through the field towards the farm buildings. Go through the gate alongside the buildings then turn left down towards the farmhouse. Now follow the hard-core track beside the river to the lane near Pontllanio. Turn right; this lane will take you back onto the B4343 just north of Llanddewibrefi.

At the road junction, go right again and continue through the village centre where you should again bear right and follow the road back to Tan-'rallt.

Lampeter
(Llanbedr Pont Steffan)

Several main roads converge at Lampeter emphasising its importance as a market and university town in the central Teifi valley.

St David's University College, originally a male preserve specialising in theology, was founded in the 19th century. In 1965 women were first admitted as students and now the emphasis is on the arts.

Llanbedr Pont Steffan – the church of St Peter by Stephen's Bridge – is the full name for the town. It has been a market town for several centuries and drovers used to meet here before leaving to walk to the markets in England. The Ram Inn, about a mile outside the town on the road to Llandovery (Llanymddyfri), is one of the original hostelries used by the drovers.

River Teifi near Cellan north of Lampeter

To appreciate Lampter it's a good idea to park the car and take a walk around the town including the back streets and lanes. Although an old settlement, much of the town's architecture dates from the 19th century.

To follow the Teifi valley down to Llanybydder take the A485 south of the town (signposted to Carmarthen). The alternative road, the A475 Newcastle Emlyn (Castellnewydd Emlyn) road, soon leaves the river behind and crosses high ground before dropping back down to the river valley near Llandyfriog.

Lampeter Walk

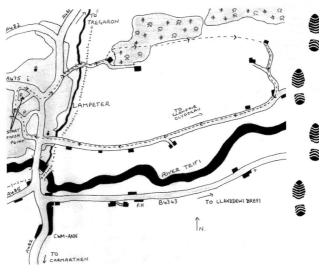

About 2½-3 hours. There is some steep climbing above the river valley and tracks may be muddy.

Park in one of the town centre car-parks and make your way on to the A482 Aberystwyth road through the town.

Walk north along the road until you reach the rugby ground on your right. If you reach the turning off to Tregaron (A485) then you have gone too far.

Walk down the track beside the rugby ground (signposted as a bridle-way), crossing a stream and passing old ruined buildings. Continue along the track, which now climbs and, at a sharp corner beside a farm, go left off the track and walk next to the farm buildings.

Go through a gap in the hedge and walk on the crown of the hill keeping the wood on your right. After a short distance turn right into the wood through a small gap then turn immediately left and walk along a stony track. Go through the gate and continue along the track to the junction. Cross the stile in front of you and walk down between a fence and a line of trees. Walk beside the wood, between old and new fences. When the track ends go right, then cross a stile. Now walk down through the field keeping the wood on your left; before reaching the end of the wood you will cross another couple of stiles. At the end of the wood, cross the stile in front of you, then head straight across the field. Now bear right and slightly downhill along the fence-line and then go through the first gate on your right and down towards the farm. Go down onto the track keeping the farm on your left and turn right along the track. Continue down the track to the lane, turn right, and follow the lane back to the main road (A482) at Lampeter. Turn right again and back to the car-park.

Llanybydder and District

There are many old and interesting churches in the Teifi valley and one of the best is at Llanwenog, a hamlet just off the A475 north of Llanybydder. The church is mainly 13th century with a tall tower; the coat of arms above the west door commemorates the victory at Bosworth in 1485. Inside, the bench ends are carved with scenes from local history beginning with Giraldus's famous journey through Wales in 1188. They are the work of 19th century sculptor,

Joseph Reubens, who was sponsored by the owners of Highmead House near Llanybydder.

The small town of Llanybydder near the banks of the river Teifi has long been known for its monthly horse sales. These sales attract buyers from all over Britain and are held on the last Thursday of every month.

South-east of the town, Mynydd Llanybydder rises to over 1300 feet (400 metres). It

Bridge below Llanllwni church

is now partly covered in commercial forestry – the northern limits of Brechfa Forest. The miles of hedgerows that are bright yellow with laburnum flowers in spring are an unusual feature of this part of Wales. A particularly good place to see this is on the B4337 Llanybydder to Llansawel road.

Llanllwni church is away from the main village, which is strung out along the main road and growing rapidly. To reach the church take any of the roads signposted to Maesycrugiau and the church is above the river on the minor road to Capel Dewi.

Llandysul

The little market town of Llandysul was once the centre of the weaving industry in Wales. The original

Llandysul church

garments were flannel shirts for workers in industrial South Wales. In recent years the industry has seen something of a revival, though not on the same scale as previously. Now the goods produced are often sold to tourists in shops in the Teifi valley or farther afield. At Dre-fach Felindre there is a museum where the whole weaving process can be observed and of course there is a shop selling goods made there. At Pont-allt-y-cafn, another village with a former mill, the high single-span bridge dates from 1839. The railway from Carmarthen served many of the mills in the valley.

Pencader, south-east of Llandysul, grew with the coming of the railway. The line from Carmarthen divided here, one branch going east to Lampeter and Tregaron and the other west to Newcastle Emlyn. Hidden among the houses in the village is a castle mound – basically a ditch surrounding a tump. It was here that Rhys ap Gruffudd paid homage to Henry II in 1163.

Llandysul church, dedicated to St Tysul, is down by the river and is typical of the Teifi valley with a tall battlemented tower. It dates from the 13th century with 15th century additions and until 1783 the church roof was thatched.

Maesycrugiau Walk

Easy, mostly level walking; allow 1-1½ hours. Park near the church hall then walk down the lane to the bridge over the Teifi. Do not cross the bridge but go

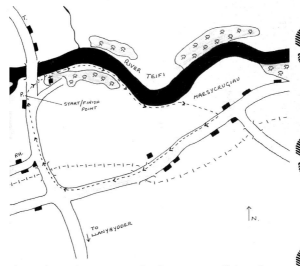

down the path on your right that runs parallel to the river. Do not take the track that bears uphill at this point as this just leads to the churchyard. Continue along the path that curves round between the river and the church. Soon you will reach an old ruined building on your right; turn left off the track through a wicket gate and go straight across the field towards the river bank. Continue through this field beside the river, go through a metal gate and now bear right, away from the river and slightly uphill towards some houses. Follow an obvious path to a wicket gate that leads out on to the lane. Turn right and follow this lane to a cross-roads, turn right again and walk down this lane back to the church hall (about a third of a mile).

Henllan

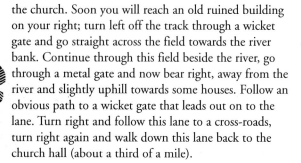

Between Llandysul and Newcastle Emlyn there are many hilltop forts and castle mounds – some easily accessible, others more difficult to find.

One of the best viewpoints in the area is Dinas Cerdin (*dinas* is Welsh for 'fort' as well as 'city'). It is about 4 miles north-west of Llandysul just near the A486 New Quay (Ceinewydd) road in beautiful hilly country.

Another hill-fort, which is not marked on many maps, is Carn Wen, about ¾ mile east of Dinas Cerdin. It includes a defensive wall of loose stones 12 feet high.

Just off the B4476 between Llandysul and Pren-gwyn there is another hill-fort, Pen-coed-y-foel, 800 feet (250 metres) above sea level.

The castle mounds in the Teifi valley date from around the 12th century. Castell Pistog is 2 miles east of Henllan at Bangor Teifi. Castell Hywel is in the Cletwr valley just off the B4459 north of Rhydowen, and Tomen Rhydowen is just south of the village. Castell

Pyr is beside the River Teifi south-west of Maesycrugiau. Most of the hill-forts and castle mounds in Wales are on private land. If there is no public footpath and if you wish to visit the sites, please find the landowner and ask permission. A polite request is not usually refused.

River Teifi at Henllan

The stretch of the Teifi that flows in a rocky gorge at Henllan is one of the most beautiful. It is spanned by a three-arched bridge that dates from 1774. Often, however, the river flows only under the southern arch.

Henllan Walk

About 1½ hours. Gentle walking beside the river, though the path is often muddy and can be slippery after rain.

Park in a lay-by near Henllan Bridge (please do not obstruct the entrance to Henllan Church and the Water Board property).

Cross the road and go down the path on the left beside a cottage. Walk next to the river along a rocky and well-worn path. Continue to follow this path,

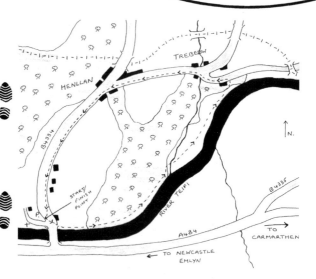

which soon leaves the river bank and now follows a
minor stream. When the path abruptly ends, cross over
the stream on your right, then turn left and follow the
hedgerow through the field. Go through the wicket gate
and head straight across the field to the stone steps next
to the metal gates.

Go up the steps passing a new house on your right
and on to the lane. Turn left and continue to bear left
until you reach a T-junction in Henllan village. Turn left
again on to B4334 and it's about another ½ mile to the
starting point of the walk.

Newcastle Emlyn
(Castellnewydd Emlyn)

The ruins of the 'new castle' stand surrounded on three sides by a loop of the river Teifi. It was built in the 13th century but all that remains today dates from the 15th century. Cromwell's soldiers blew up the original castle with great effect and it was then rebuilt as a fortified residence.

The castle grounds are open to the public and are a popular place for picnics. Beside the castle car-park there used to be a mill near where the modern Roman Catholic church now stands. In the river below the castle can be seen remnants of a dam used to divert water into the mill-leat easily visible between river and castle mound. Newcastle Emlyn is a market town consisting mainly of one long street, quiet except on Fridays – market day.

Between Lampeter and Cardigan the river forms the boundary between the counties of Carmarthenshire and Ceredigion. County pride has in the past

The castle at Newcastle Emlyn

been fierce between the towns and villages on opposite banks of the river.

Newcastle Emlyn was in Carmarthenshire and Adpar, over the bridge, refused to be included in the urban district when it was created in 1897.

The first printing press in Wales was set up at Adpar in 1718 by Isaac Carter.

Cenarth

Pub at Cenarth, complete with coracle

Cenarth is a village on the A484 Carmarthen to Cardigan road. Out of season it is quiet but in summer it is packed with cars and coach-loads of visitors. Severe congestion is caused by the narrow 18th century bridge over the Teifi. It is built in the style of William Edwards, with circular openings on each side to relieve flood waters. A good example of a genuine Edwards bridge is over the Tywi at Dolauhirion near Llandovery.

There are lovely picturesque falls near the bridge and, beside the river, a restored flour-mill. In the grounds of the mill is the National Coracle Centre of Wales. On display are coracles from all over the world as well as craft from other parts of Wales. Visitors can watch coracles being made and sometimes see them in use on the river. The Teifi and the Tywi are the only two rivers in Wales where coracles are regularly used for fishing.

Cenarth church is on a hill overlooking the river and contains a 13th century font. The village itself is very much geared to the tourist trade. There are craft shops, tearooms and a café catering for coach parties.

A road (signposted to Boncath) leads south-west to the valley of the River Cuch. It is a beautiful, peaceful, wooded valley, where you can escape from the crowds at Cenarth. This area was once a stronghold of wood turners and carvers. Welsh love-spoons were a speciality.

Manordeifi/Llechryd

The old church at Manordeifi is close to the south bank of the Teifi. It was so often flooded in the past that it was equipped with its own coracle for rescuing the prayer-books as the waters rose. It has a medieval font and two of the box pews at the front of the church are fitted with fireplaces – strictly for the gentry.

In the church there is a monument to Captain Charles Colby of the 98th Regiment whose family owned Ffynone near Aber-cuch. He died in 1852 at Rawalpindi after falling victim to a tiger.

Ffynone was one of many fine gentlemen's residences in the Teifi valley between Lampeter and Cardigan. Why this part of Wales was so popular with the gentry in the 18th and 19th centuries is not entirely clear. Perhaps it was because it was within easy reach of Cardigan – at that

Manordeifi church

time a major port – and therefore there was easy access to South Wales, Bristol and the West of England. Ffynone was one of the finest examples in the valley, built in the 1790s by John Nash, with two wings added in the 1920s. Between 1902 and 1907 the house was enlarged and altered by Inigo Thomas. Extensive woodlands surround the house.

The bridge over the Teifi at Llechryd is ancient. There is a date (1695) on the upstream side but, as with many dates inscribed on old bridges, this could just be the date of a repair.

Castell Malgwyn Hotel on the river bank was the site of a tinplate works owned by Sir Benjamin Hammet. A leat ran from the river Teifi below Manordeifi church to the works, providing water power.

Cilgerran

Cilgerran is a pleasant Teifiside village, formerly a borough that had the benefit of being on the railway line from Cardigan down to south Pembrokeshire. The main street is wide and tree-lined giving an air of quiet prosperity. One or two shops serve the local community and many more people during the holiday season.

The remains of a Norman castle stand high above the river, mostly now consisting of two great towers and a massive gate house from the 13th century. It has been popular with artists through the centuries including Turner who painted the castle in 1799. Down near the castle is a small coracle museum.

On the western edge of the village St Llawdog's church is mainly 19th century with a 13th century tower.

A beautiful riverside walk leads to the bridge at Llechryd. Near the walk are the remains of quarries and information boards nearby give details of their long history. Slate from these quarries is much in evidence inside and outside the church at Newcastle Emlyn.

Near Cilgerran, the Teifi becomes tidal and flows between wooded banks and more quarries. Just to the east of Cardigan is a reserve of

Riverside walk near Cilgerran

the West Wales Wildlife Trust. This is the Teifi Marshes and, as the name suggests, it is an area of marshes and reeds beside the tidal Teifi. To reach the reserve follow the signs from Cardigan. The reserve is about 2½ miles outside the town and off the A478 to Narberth.

Cilgerran Walk

Allow about 2 hours for this easy riverside walk, though the path may occasionally be muddy.

In Cilgerran park down by the river where there are picnic tables and public toilets. If the riverside car-park is full, there is further car parking available just south of the village on the road to Boncath or a little farther out on the minor road to Cardigan. Follow the path down

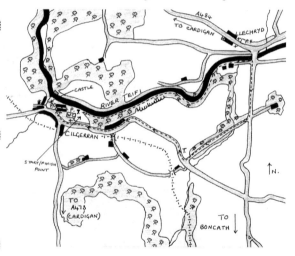

to the river signposted to Llechryd (2 miles). Continue along this well-used path, always keeping close to the river bank. In one place where the path forks, you should take the lower fork and follow the yellow arrows to Llechryd Bridge.

On reaching the bridge, turn right and walk up this road to the first turning on the right. Follow this lane down to the T-junction beside the phone box, turn right again and walk back to Cilgerran. In the village turn down a steep lane beside the shop signposted 'to the river'.

Cardigan

The Welsh name for Cardigan is Aberteifi, reflecting its position at the mouth of the river Teifi. For several centuries it was one of the busiest ports in Wales and the old warehouses can still be seen on the quayside today. In the first half of the 19th century the port was the departure point for ships taking emigrants to Canada and New York State. In St Mary's churchyard there are many graves of 18th and 19th century sailors. In

Upriver to Cardigan bridge

common with other ports in Wales, sea trade declined dramatically with the arrival of the railway in 1885.

The ruined castle stands near the river. It was rebuilt by Gilbert Marshal (son of the Earl of Pembroke) and finally ruined by Cromwell's troops. The original castle is believed to have been the venue of the first National Eisteddfod in 1176 with Lord Rhys of Deheubarth as host.

137

St Mary's church was largely rebuilt at the beginning of the 18th century but has many features from earlier times.

The multi-arched bridge over the Teifi has pedestrian passing places and the date 1726 on one of the arches. Cardigan today is a thriving market town with a general market and livestock sales at a site just outside the town.

Just off the coast near the mouth of the Teifi is Cardigan Island, another West Wales Wildlife Trust reserve and a haven for seabirds. For details of trips to the island and any other information about the WWWT you should contact the Trust office in Haverfordwest (Hwlffordd).

St Dogmaels (Llandudoch)

St Dogmaels or Llandudoch is a fishing village a mile west of Cardigan. The estuary is hidden from the main road through the village by trees and many of the houses hug the wooded slopes overlooking the river.

Just off the main street is St Dogmaels Abbey; it was founded in 1115 by twelve monks and a prior from Tiron in France by order of Robert Martin Lord of Cemaes. The ruins, which are open to the public, date mostly from the 14th and 15th centuries. Next to the Abbey the parish church of St Thomas the Martyr was built in 1847 and contains a 7 foot stone pillar with an Ogham inscription on one edge. This stone supplied the key to the interpretation of the Ogham alphabet in 1848.

Opposite St Dogmaels at Old Castle Farm there was a castle until the 13th century when it was replaced by the one near the Teifi Bridge at Cardigan.

Near the mouth of the Teifi estuary, Gwbert on Sea consists mainly of a large hotel, holiday parks and golf links.

The cliffs at Gwbert are home in summer to house-martins who nest on the side of the cliffs. In May the grassy cliff tops are patched blue with spring squill, a low-growing star-shaped flower.

The Ferry Inn, St Dogmaels

Teifi Estuary

Beyond St Dogmaels the Teifi estuary widens and salty creeks and marshes give way to sandy beaches at Poppit. Visitors are well catered for here with car-parks, refreshment kiosks and public conveniences. Next to the Lifeboat Station is the Surf Life Saving Club. A more usual sight on American and Australian beaches, it is however a comfort to the thousands of families who visit the beach during the season.

There is a large caravan park along the road to Moylgrove (Trewyddel) and a youth hostel half a mile from the beach car-parks.

The narrow lane up to the hostel eventually peters out

The Teifi Estuary near Old Castle Farm

and here begins the 180 mile Pembrokeshire Coast Path. Apart from a few breaks, the path is continuous to Amroth, north of Tenby (Dinbych-y-pysgod). The path is waymarked by acorns on wooden posts and quite easy to follow. Much of the coastline is rugged and the cliffs high so take care not to venture too close to the cliff edge especially if it's windy.

Cemaes Head, where the Poppit road ends, is the most northerly tip of the Pembrokeshire Coast National Park. The Park was designated in 1952 and covers 225 square miles (582 square kilometres). No part of the Park is more than 10 miles (16 kilometres) from the sea. One of the best inland features of the Park is the Preseli hills almost due south of Cemaes Head. Here on the bleak, windy hills there is an amazing concentration of cairns, burial chambers and standing stones – evidence of prehistoric man's activity in the area.

Poppit Walk

Allow yourself up to 2 hours for this walk, which is steep in places, particularly the first half.

Park in one of the several car-parks on Poppit Sands. Walk up the lane past a refreshment kiosk following signs for the Youth Hostel. Continue up this steep narrow lane, which is a dead end for traffic, until you reach the Youth Hostel (half a mile). Just past the

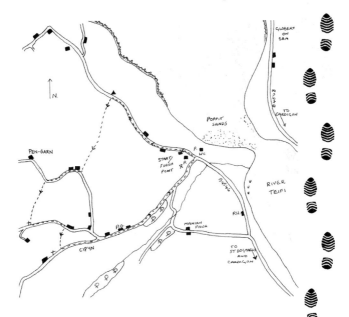

entrance to the Hostel cross the stile in the hedge on your left. Walk straight up the field alongside an old hedge bank, cross the stile next to the gate and continue to the next stile. Cross the stile, turn right and head towards the farm. Just before reaching the buildings cross another stile on to the farm track, and keeping the buildings on your right continue down the track now posted a bridle-way. When the track turns sharply right, go through the gate on your left and follow a grassy track between gorse and hedge bank around the side of the hill. Continue downhill to a metal gate, go through the gate and down a rough path towards an old chapel. Turn left down the track past the chapel, continue through a farmyard, then just past the buildings, go through a gate on your right. Walk down through the field then uphill towards another chapel on the horizon (the path here may be overgrown between the old hedges). Go through a metal gate on to the lane, turn left and follow back to Poppit passing through the hamlet of Cipin on the way. From here it's about one mile back to the car-parks and the start of the walk.

River
TYWI

Introduction

The area of Wales through which the river Tywi flows is easily accessible by road and rail and has in recent years become a popular holiday destination.

The main town on the river, Carmarthen (Caerfyrddin), is around 250 miles from London and the South-East of England and there is a dual carriageway from the western end of the M4 to the town.

The other towns are all on the A40 Carmarthen to Brecon (Aberhonddu) road. There are railway links from Swansea (Abertawe) to Carmarthen and the Heart of Wales line runs from Swansea north through Llandeilo and Llandovery (Llanymddyfri) and on to Shrewsbury.

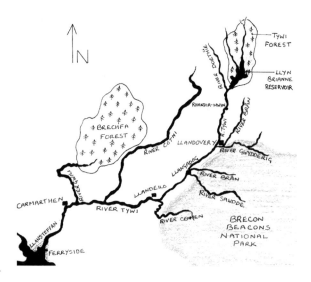

For visitors to the area accommodation ranges from grand country hotels to youth hostels high up in the hills. For hardier souls who do not mind braving the weather, there are several campsites near the banks of the river.

From its humble beginnings 1500 feet (460 metres) up in the Cambrian mountains to the wide expanse of Carmarthen Bay where it meets the sea, the river Tywi flows for most of its 68 miles through an almost wholly rural landscape. The area is well suited for outdoor activities such as fishing, pony-trekking and walking.

For serious walkers, it is the upper Tywi valley north of Rhandir-mwyn that provides the greatest challenge and of course the Brecon Beacons (Bannau Brycheiniog) are only a few miles away.

However, all the walks described in this chapter are easy and should present no problems for even the most 'occasional' walker.

OS maps covering the river Tywi area are 159, 146, 147 in the Landranger 1:50 000 series.

Llyn Brianne and the Tywi Forest

The minor road from Llandovery through Rhandir-mwyn to Tregaron, following the eastern shore of Llyn Brianne, provides panoramic views across the reservoir and the conifer plantations known as the Tywi Forest. The Forestry Commission has established several picnic sites near the roadside. The Commission allows pedestrian access through most of its plantations but you should observe local signs as, occasionally, areas are closed to the public when felling or other work is in progress. You may encounter sheep wandering along the road so drive carefully especially at lambing time.

Soar-y-mynydd chapel near the banks of the river Camddwr was built in 1822 and holds services during the summer.

River Camddwr above Llyn Brianne

The road from Tregaron to Llanwrtyd (Wells) which crosses the River Tywi near the Dol-goch Youth Hostel is the old drovers' road. Livestock from Mid Wales often had to travel as far as London and Essex and blacksmiths along the route did a good trade shoeing cattle.

The source of the river Tywi can only be reached on foot. Park on the minor road near Ty'n-cwm Farm about a mile and a half from Strata Florida Abbey (see River Teifi). Walk down the farm track then continue in an easterly direction across the mountain. There is no pathway to the spring that is the source of the river and you will need permission from the landowner and a compass to find it, using OS map sheet 147. However if you enjoy mountain walking then it is well worth the effort. Remember though that this is a walk where you reach 1700 feet (500 metres) above sea level so go well prepared for all weathers.

Llyn Brianne

In the early 1970s a huge reservoir was constructed in the Upper Tywi valley to provide water for Swansea and the rest of West Glamorgan. The area was ideal because of its high rainfall, remoteness and lack of human habitation.

The spillway at the southern end of the reservoir is 165 feet (150 metres) long and is used as an overflow; consequently it is dry for much of the summer. There are public car-parks at the top and bottom of the spillway.

Spillway at Llyn Brianne

The reservoir is not used for recreational purposes such as fishing and boating as the cost of providing a safe environment for those taking part would be excessive in such a potentially dangerous area. It would also spoil the general public's enjoyment of this alien but visually stunning landscape.

During the severe drought of 1995 the water level in the reservoir fell to such an extent that old farm buildings and stone walls were exposed.

Twm Siôn Cati and the Monks of Strata Florida

Every part of Wales has its legends and the upper Tywi valley is no exception. Up a steep path in the Dinas nature reserve there is a cave formed by the collapse of several large boulders. The entrance is narrow and the roof open to the sky. This, according to legend and the graffiti of centuries, is Ystafell Twm Siôn Cati (Twm Siôn Cati's Room).

There are many stories about Twm and some liken him to Robin Hood of England. Twm was a real person,

St Paulinus's church near the Dinas Nature Reserve

born in Tregaron in 1530, who took his unmarried mother's name – Thomas John (son of) Catherine. He came from aristocratic stock and certainly had no need to steal sheep, but as a young man he was outlawed and then, for reasons unknown, given a royal pardon in 1559. He became a highly acclaimed scholar, poet and genealogist. Many fine examples of his work remain today.

Late in life he married the widow of the High

Sheriff of Carmarthenshire who lived at Ystrad-ffin farm near the Dinas reserve. There is no proof that Twm actually spent any time at the cave.

St Paulinus's church, adjacent to the Dinas, was established in the 12th century by monks from Strata Florida Abbey (see River Teifi) who used to pass this way as they travelled with their livestock to the market at Neath (Castell-nedd).

The church was rebuilt by order of Lord Cawdor in the 19th century and completely restored in 1984 by an MSC team. Services are held throughout the year.

Gwenffrwd Dinas Nature Reserve

Lush wooded river valleys and high bracken-covered hills make up the RSPB's Gwenffrwd Dinas Reserve in the upper Tywi valley. 'Hanging' sessile oak-woods clothe the steep slopes of the Dinas hill and, nearer the base, birch grows alongside the oaks. In the damper places alder is a dominant species.

In spring and early summer the woodland is alive with birds and many nest boxes have been erected to encourage them. Pied flycatchers in particular have benefited from the siting of the boxes as their numbers have increased dramatically in recent years. Other woodland species to look out for include redstarts, willow warblers and several members of the tit family. Green and Great Spotted woodpeckers can also be seen on the reserve. Riverside birds that are regularly spotted include sandpipers, dippers and goosanders.

The Dinas Nature Reserve north of Rhandir-mwyn

In winter the woods may be a little quieter but there are usually flocks of tits feeding with nut-hatches and treecreepers.

Larger birds to be seen in and around the reserve throughout the year include buzzards, ravens, sparrow-hawks and the rare red kite.

The Gwenffrwd is mostly heather and bracken-covered moorland rising to 1500 feet (460 metres) above the rivers Tywi and Doethïe. This part of the reserve can only be visited after first obtaining a permit from the warden or the Dinas Visitors' Centre. Much more information on the nature of the upper Tywi valley can be obtained from the visitors' centre.

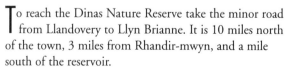

Dinas Reserve Walk

To reach the Dinas Nature Reserve take the minor road from Llandovery to Llyn Brianne. It is 10 miles north of the town, 3 miles from Rhandir-mwyn, and a mile south of the reservoir.

From the car-park next to St Paulinus's church follow the boardwalk through an area of marshy

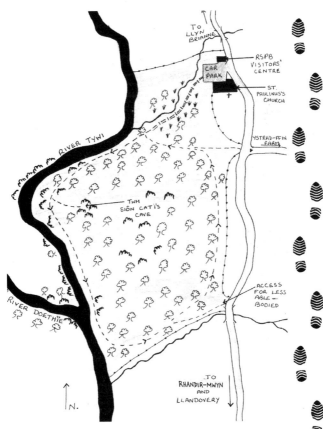

Map labels:
TO LLYN BRIANNE
RSPB VISITORS' CENTRE
CAR PARK
ST. PAULINUS'S CHURCH
RIVER TYWI
YSTRAD-FFIN FARM
TWM SIÔN CATI'S CAVE
ACCESS FOR LESS ABLE-BODIED
RIVER DOETHIE
TO RHANDIR-MWYN AND LLANDOVERY
N.

ground. When the boardwalk ends the path drops down
to the bank of the River Tywi and begins its circuit
around the hill. At this point the path climbs and
becomes rocky. It is well worth a bit of a scramble but
take care and wear sensible shoes or boots as the rocks
can be very slippery, particularly after wet weather.

About two-thirds of the way around the western side

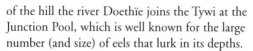

of the hill the river Doethïe joins the Tywi at the Junction Pool, which is well known for the large number (and size) of eels that lurk in its depths.

Leaving the Junction Pool behind, the path continues around the hill, but walking gradually becomes a little easier. When it reaches the south-east corner of the reserve the path follows the road and a grassy track takes you through part of the reserve that is particularly beautiful during spring and early summer.

The path soon meets up with the boardwalk to take you back to the car-park.

The whole circuit takes 1-1½ hours.

Rhandir-mwyn and the Upper Tywi Valley

As the largest village in the upper Tywi valley, Rhandir-mwyn is now geared up for the increasing number of visitors to the area, including walkers and cyclists staying at the nearby youth hostel. There are several campsites within easy reach of the village and some local farms and inns provide accommodation.

In common with much of upland Wales, Rhandir-mwyn was important in the lead-mining industry. There are footpaths from the post office through conifer plantations to the remains of the mines on the hillside above the village.

Between Rhandir-mwyn and Llandovery the river Tywi flows through a wooded valley and is joined by many mountain streams. The area is popular with fishermen.

About 1½ miles from Rhandir-mwyn on the road to Cil-y-cwm the Forestry Commission has established a picnic site in a conifer plantation. From here there is an excellent walk up to Cwm y Rhaeadr waterfall – the walk takes about 1½ hours.

Cil-y-cwm is an attractive village well worth a visit, with its cobbled culverts and colour-washed cottages and chapel. The church is one of the best in the area

River Tywi near Rhandir-mwyn

and is a mixture of 13th and 15th century architecture.

The wildlife of the upper Tywi is varied, the native woodlands in the valley bottom being most rewarding for birds and wild flowers in spring and early summer. Over the higher hills the buzzards, ravens and red kites can be seen throughout the year.

Rhandir-mwyn Walk

Allow 3-3½ hours for the walk; mostly level walking except for some steep steps through the woodland.

Park in the village centre and walk down the lane opposite the post office. Pass the entrance to the campsite and cross the stile just before the bridge across

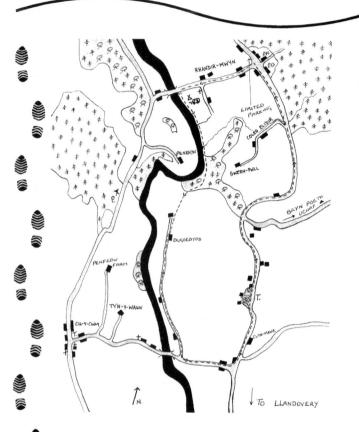

the River Tywi. Walk alongside the river through the
campsite then cross a stile. Continue to follow the river
bank, then cross over a small stream. The footpath here
is marked by boulders painted yellow. Over another
stream the path now begins to climb by way of several
steps. Cross a stile and now the path climbs high above
the river, through a wood – a long series of steps has
been constructed to make the climb a little easier. At the

top, climb the stile, turn right, go down the bank, and
cross the stile at the bottom. Bear left towards a house,
climb a stile under a large tree and walk along the edge
of the field. Leaving the house on your right, turn left
down the farm track and follow this to the farm
(Dugoedydd). Turn right in to the lane opposite the
farmyard and follow the river until you come to a road
junction. This lane connects the Cil-y-cwm road to the
Rhandir-mwyn road. Turn left and walk up to the
junction. Turn left again and from here it's about 3
miles back to Rhandir-mwyn.

Llandovery (Llanymddyfri)

Llandovery in the
upper Tywi valley has
the reputation for being
more Irish than Welsh.
This might be because of
the relaxed, friendly
atmosphere as much as
the large number of pubs
and inns in the town!

It is a bustling market
town on the A40 to
Brecon and the Heart of
Wales railway line runs
through the town and on
to Builth Wells (Llanfair-
ym-Muallt).

The remains of the
castle are on a mound

*Dolauhirion bridge over the
River Tywi near Llandovery*

near the bank of the River Gwydderig within the town car-park and a playground and picnic site have been established here.

The town has the distinction of having, in Llandovery College, one of the best public schools in Wales.

Hotels, inns and guest-houses in and around the town provide a variety of accommodation and there is a camping and caravan site less than a mile outside town on the Brecon road. The world renowned hymn writer William Williams lived near Llandovery and the 19th century traveller George Borrow sang the praises of the town in his book *Wild Wales.* Llandovery provides an ideal base for exploring the upper Tywi valley and the reservoirs of the Elan Valley are less than 35 miles away.

Llandovery Walk

This walk follows riverside paths to the north and south of the A40 bridge over the River Tywi and can be done as two separate walks. There is parking in Llandovery town centre.

Allow about 2½ hours to complete the walk; the paths and field tracks may be muddy.

From the car-park walk up the A483 Builth Wells road, then take the turning off to the left signposted to Rhandir-mwyn. Continue for approximately one mile until you reach a left turn. Go down this lane, then, just before crossing the bridge over the Tywi, go over the stile on your left and down into the field. Follow the river bank until you come to a stream flowing into the river. Turn left and walk next to the stream, cross the

first stile you come to, continue beside the stream, then
cross the wooden footbridge. Head straight towards the
farmhouse, then, keeping the house between yourself
and the river, bear left through the farm gate, go across
the track and over a stile. Follow the fence-line, then
bear right under a large tree and over another stile on to

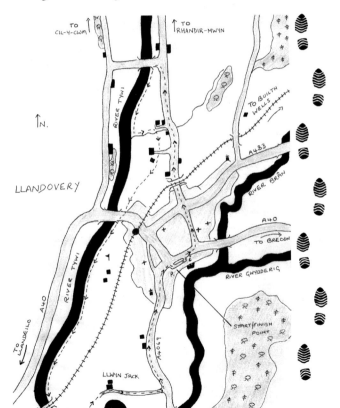

the remnants of an old track between hedges. Soon the
river will again come into view and now you should
continue parallel to the river whilst heading towards the
house by slightly bearing left across the field. Go over
the stile and, taking great care, cross the A40. Turn right
towards the bridge, then go over the awkward block stile
and into the field. Walk down beside the river and
follow the river bank past the cricket ground, through
the golf-course and the back of the rugby club until
yellow arrows on wooden posts direct you slightly away
from the river. Continue parallel to the river under the
railway bridge and then bear away from the river and up
the track towards the farmyard. Make your way through
the farmyard keeping the house to your left and go onto
the farm track. Follow the track down to the main road
(A4069), turn left, and walk back towards Llandovery
(approximately 1 mile). On reaching the town centre,
turn right and the car-park is on your right.

Llansadwrn and Llanwrda

Between the towns of Llandovery and Llandeilo the
River Tywi meanders through an ever-widening
valley overlooked by steep hills both to the east and
west.

   Up in the hills to the north of Llangadog is the
beautifully sited village of Llansadwrn. It comprises all the
essential ingredients of a Welsh village – a little post office,
an inn, a couple of chapels and a church. All this and
panoramic views across the Tywi valley to the Brecon
Beacons. There are numerous quiet lanes, tracks and paths
to explore which lead farther up into the hills. One of the

best viewpoints in the area is at the site of an Iron Age fort on the hill known as Y Fan about 1½ miles west of the village.

Back down in the valley, the village of Llanwrda is split by the busy A40 road. The tiny railway station, an inn and an old water-mill (hopefully soon to be restored) are on the river side of the road. The main part of the village is opposite and from here the A482 to Lampeter follows the Roman road as far as Pumsaint. The

Llansadwrn church high above the Tywi valley

Roman road then heads due north to join the Teifi valley a few miles from Lampeter at Llanfair Clydogau.

Llangadog

Much of Llangadog's prosperity has been brought about by a number of industries on the outskirts of the town. As you would expect most of these are linked to the farming aspect of the Tywi valley – a creamery, concrete works, and a timber sawmill all cater for the agricultural needs of the area.

The Tywi itself does not actually flow through Llangadog but passes to the west of the town where it is joined by a major tributary, the Sawdde. This is a fast-flowing river that has its source at Llyn y Fan Fach, a lake high up in the Brecon Beacons National Park.

Llangadog is a mixture of old and new. The main street is lined with colour-washed buildings that make it seem narrower than it really is, and the Red Lion Inn is where Oliver Cromwell is reputed to have stayed.

About 3 miles south-west, the village of Bethlehem is well known for its specially post-marked Christmas mail. On a hill overlooking the village is Garn Goch, one of the largest Iron Age hill-forts in Wales.

River Tywi near Llangadog

The western edge of the Brecons is right on your doorstep in this part of the Tywi valley, and from the youth hostel at Llanddeusant some of the most spectacular scenery in southern Britain can be reached on foot within a couple of hours.

Llangadog Walk

Allow at least 3 hours; a couple of small inclines, fields and tracks will probably be muddy. There is limited parking at Llangadog common, about ½ mile on the road to Brynaman.

Walk down on to the town side of the common and follow the grassy track parallel to the river until a wire

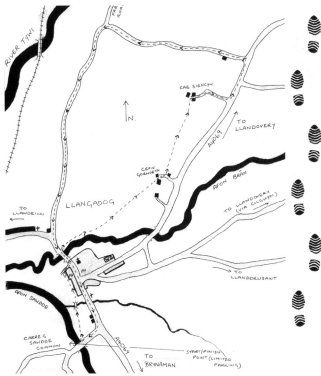

fence bars the way. Bear right, cross a ditch and then a footbridge over a stream. Go through the wicket gate and into the field. Walk diagonally across to the next gateway and then head up towards buildings in the top left-hand corner of the field. Go round the buildings on to the track and continue ahead to the main road. Turn left and then, just over the hump bridge, turn right down to the river bank (Afon Brân). Follow the path alongside the river and continue, passing through a couple more gates and crossing a stream, until you reach the field corner. Turn left away from the river and follow the hedge until you come to a gap. Go straight ahead up through the field and through the next gap in the hedge. Continue uphill towards a big house, then, keeping the house and farm buildings on your left, go through a gate and into the yard. Now bear left onto the farm track and walk down until you reach a sharp corner near a new bungalow. Go through the gate on the left and follow the fence-line uphill, then go through the gap in the hedge-line on your left. Now continue in this same direction (parallel to the main road) until you see a farm in the dip ahead. Before reaching the farm bear left along the hedge and go through a metal gate to take you into the farmyard. Go down to join the farm lane and continue along here until you reach the main road (A4069). Turn left and walk along the verge, then take the first lane on the left. Follow this lane for approximately 2 miles until you find yourself back in Llangadog. Turn left, then, in the village centre, follow the signs to Brynaman and you will reach the common in about ½ mile.

Llandeilo

Like Llandovery,
Llandeilo is a market
town on the A40 and the
Heart of Wales line runs
through the town with
stations at Ffair-fach and
Llandeilo. It is situated in
a central position in the
beautiful Vale of Tywi
(Dyffryn Tywi) with easy
access to South and West
Wales (Carmarthen is 15
miles away).

*Dinefwr Castle and
Park near Llandeilo*

The parish church of
St Teilo is mainly 19th
century although the
tower is a fine example of
13th century
architecture. In the
churchyard wall a grotto conceals a well, once believed
to have healing properties.

The stone bridge across the river Tywi was built in
1848 and is said to be the longest and highest single-
span bridge in Wales.

The National Trust has its South Wales headquarters
here in the old King's Head and owns the nearby
Dinefwr (Dynevor) Park. Part of the park was presented
to the town for use as an amenity – this is known as
Pen-lan Park and is a landmark with its two clumps of
beech trees on the horizon.

Dinefwr Castle, which is high above the river Tywi, was built in the 12th century and was the seat of the Princes of the old Welsh kingdom of Deheubarth (the South).

Castle Woods nature reserve covers 62 acres and is owned by the West Wales Wildlife Trust. It is a short walk from the town centre – either through Pen-lan Park or from near the Tywi Bridge – and consists of mixed woodland, some of which clings to the steep slopes below Dinefwr Castle. It is a Site of Special Scientific Interest and particularly important for lichens and mosses. Llandyfeisant church, within the reserve, is used as a visitors' centre and is open from Easter to September.

About 4 miles from Llandeilo is Carreg Cennen castle perched on a hill above the village of Trap.

Pont-bren Araeth (Llandeilo) Walk

This walk follows tracks and lanes high above the Tywi valley giving panoramic views across and along the valley and also good views of Garn Goch Iron age hill-fort to the east.

Allow 2½-3 hours; some steep climbs – tracks and paths could be muddy.

Limited roadside parking is available at Pont-bren Araeth (about 3 miles out of Llandeilo on the road to Bethlehem).

From the parking place walk back down to the river, cross the bridge, and turn down the tarmac lane on your

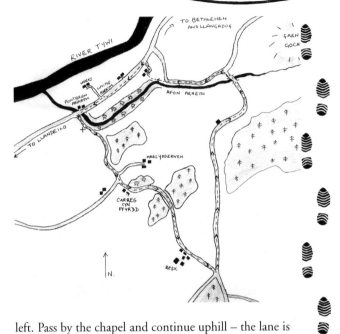

left. Pass by the chapel and continue uphill – the lane is now a track, often muddy and overgrown. Follow this for about ¾ mile until you rejoin a tarmac lane. Turn right then left at the first junction. Now follow this road for 1 mile until you reach a four-way junction. Turn left and follow the road downhill passing new plantations on your right. Cross over the Araeth and now, on your right, you will have a good view of Garn Goch. Continue to the junction, turn left, and follow the road for about ½ mile to a sharp right-hand bend. Cross the stile on your left and walk straight ahead through the scrubby woodland. Continue beside the river till you reach a ford, then bear right onto a well-worn track and continue towards farm buildings. Go over a ladder stile and turn right down the farm track and out onto the road. Turn left and in about ½ mile you will reach the parking place.

Gelli-aur (Golden Grove) and Llangathen

The grounds of Gelli-aur mansion, once the home of the Vaughan family, are now a country park owned by Carmarthenshire County Council.

Three miles west of Llandeilo on the B4300 to Carmarthen, it is a popular place for locals and holidaymakers to visit throughout the year.

The arboretum has splendid trees and shrubs from around the world. There is also a breeding herd of fallow deer and nature trails through the woodland.

A picnic site and children's play area have been constructed and there is a visitors' centre with a cafeteria.

The mansion at Gelli-aur is now part of the local agricultural college. Across the river Tywi via Cilsan Bridge is the small

The visitors' centre at Gelli-aur

hamlet of Llangathen. The village has an interesting
church with a 13th century tower and inside there are
effigies of Bishop Rudd who lived with his wife at
Aberglasney House. Now, sadly, a ruin, Aberglasney was
where the poet and painter John Dyer spent his
childhood. The once magnificent gardens are now in
the hands of the Welsh Historic Gardens Trust who are
hoping to restore them to their former glory.

The Tywi Valley near Dryslwyn Castle

The Tywi valley between
Llandeilo and
Carmarthen is lush and
green, which makes it
good grazing land. There
are many dairy farms in
this part of the valley.
The flooding that can
occur at any time of year,
and sometimes turns the
whole valley floor into a
huge lake, makes the soil
very rich.

Dryslwyn Castle

At Dryslwyn, about 6
miles from Llandeilo, the
remains of a castle stand
on a knoll next to the
river Tywi. This castle was
built by the English in

the 13th century and is in a strategic position between the Norman centre at Carmarthen and the Welsh stronghold of Dinefwr (Llandeilo).

Below the castle there is a car-park and picnic site and boards with more information about the Tywi valley and surrounding area.

During the winter, white fronted geese from Greenland and several species of duck can be seen on the river and in the pools near the castle.

Middleton Hall and Paxton's Tower

Decorative waterfall at Middleton Hall

Overlooking the village of Llanarthne in the mid Tywi valley is a folly known as Paxton's Tower. Sir William Paxton commissioned the tower to commemorate Nelson's victory at the Battle of Trafalgar. The tower is signposted from Llanarthne, which is on the B4300 from Llandeilo to Carmarthen. The National Trust has owned the tower and the surrounding field since 1965 and a walk up to the top of the hill will be rewarded with panoramic views north, south, east and west.

About 1½ miles from Llanarthne on the road to Llanddarog, the grounds of Middleton Hall (formerly the home of Sir William Paxton) have been opened to the public. Like Aberglasney at Llangathen they are being restored by the Welsh Historic Gardens Trust. It is a particularly beautiful area in spring and early summer. There is roadside parking and information boards give more details about the history and natural history of the estate.

A multi-million pound grant has recently been received and work is in progress on establishing a National Botanic Garden at Middleton Hall. Planners hope it will eventually rival Kew Gardens in London.

Nantgaredig and the River Cothi

The River Cothi is the major tributary of the Tywi and has its source 1200 feet (365 metres) up in the hills about 6 miles west of the Dinas nature reserve.

Until it reaches Pontargothi, very close to its meeting point with the Tywi, the Cothi has the characteristics of an upland river, never meandering gently through lush pastures but hurrying over rocks and through steep narrow gorges.

Near Pumsaint on the A482 Llanwrda to Lampeter road, the river flows by the Dolaucothi gold mines believed to have been worked since Roman times and

Afon Clydach in Brechfa Forest – one of the many streams that flow into the Cothi, itself a tributary of the Tywi

now owned by the National Trust and open to the public.

On the B4302 from Llandeilo to Llansawel is the village of Talley (Talyllychau) with its ruined 12th century abbey and twin lakes. Nearby, the river Cothi skirts Brechfa Forest with its many picnic sites and forest walks.

The Cothi is considered by many fishermen to be superior to the Tywi due to the high levels of acidity recorded in the Upper Tywi valley, particularly around Llyn Brianne. However, in recent years, efforts have been made to reverse this situation and hopefully the Tywi will regain its reputation as one of the best sea-trout (sewin) rivers in Britain.

From the three-arched, stone packhorse bridge near Nantgaredig there is access to the banks of the Tywi and a public footpath from here takes you through fields and out onto the A40 about a mile west of the village. However if you do decide to attempt the walk, take care as the A40 is quite narrow and there is no pavement back to Nantgaredig.

Carmarthen (Caerfyrddin)

Carmarthen is regarded as the Gateway to West Wales and is the administrative centre for the county.

There has been a town here since Roman times and a settlement predating that by several centuries.

It has had a turbulent history, being the centre of many sieges and battles. Carmarthen Castle was built high above the river Tywi where County Hall now stands. There is not much to be seen now but quite a lot of the castle gateway remains just off Nott Square. Much of the old town still remains with its narrow, steep streets but, with an ever increasing volume of holiday and commercial traffic, a bypass is planned to ease the already considerable congestion.

Carmarthen, being on the estuary of the river Tywi, was once a thriving port but, with the coming of the railway to the town in the 19th century, trade declined and now the quay is used only for pleasure craft.

Almost circular boats called coracles were first used by fishermen on the Tywi before Roman times and are still used today

River Tywi near the village of Abergwili, west of Carmarthen

though only by special licence. They are still in use on the river Teifi near Cenarth.

There are good facilities and plenty of accommodation of every kind in and around the town for visitors.

Just outside Carmarthen on the A40 at Abergwili is the county museum, which displays relics from as far afield as Tibet and Egypt as well as from local sites.

About a mile east of Abergwili is Merlin's Hill. A footpath leads up the steep wooded hill believed to have associations with the magician and sage of Arthurian legend.

Llansteffan Walk

Allow about 1 hour for the walk although you may want to visit the castle on the way round. Apart from the steps near the beginning of the walk, it is mostly easy going on tracks and paths that will be muddy at times.

Parking is available at either end of 'The Green' opposite the beach in Llansteffan. If the tide is low enough, walk along the beach to a series of stone steps amongst the rocks. Climb these steps and go left along the well-worn path.

If the tide is too high, walk from the car-park to the narrow lane (marked on the map), go up the lane until you see some steps on your left. Climb these then follow the path through the woodland until you eventually meet up with the top of the beach steps. Continue along the cliff-top path until it divides. Take the right-hand fork and follow this path until it, too, divides.

Here you must take the lower path, which leads down
to the rocky foreshore where a stream flows into the sea.
Walk up from the beach, and keeping the house on your
left, go up the track and through a gate. Continue along
the track, go through another gate and out onto a lane
near another house. Follow this lane steeply uphill until
it levels out. If you wish to visit the castle, continue
along this lane and you will soon reach a track
signposted to the castle (on your right).

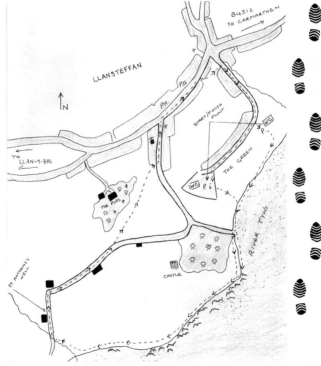

If you do not wish to visit the castle, cross over a stile hidden in a dip on the left side of the lane just before it takes a sharp turn to the right. Walk down through the field keeping the old wall and then the woodland on your left. Go over the brow of the hill and down to the bottom left-hand corner of the field. Go down the steps and onto the road and turn left to reach a T-junction. Turn right and walk through the village until the pavement peters out and you will see a signposted footpath on your right. Follow the path down between the hedges and into the housing estate. Once on the road, turn right to return to the beachside car-parks.

The Estuary of the River Tywi

The villages of Llansteffan and Ferryside (Glanyferi) are on opposite sides of the Tywi estuary and both are popular holiday spots.

Llansteffan is the larger of the two villages with extensive sands at low tide. It is well equipped for the holiday trade with a caravan park near the village centre.

Ferryside is on the east bank of the estuary and can be reached from the A484 Llanelli to Carmarthen road. Turn off in the town of Kidwelly (Cydweli).

It has the advantage of being on the railway route from Swansea to West Wales and has its own tiny station.

There is a church and two chapels in the village and the little church of St Ishmael stands alongside the

railway line near the
estuary and just outside
the village.

Carmarthen Bay is
important for the large
numbers of wildfowl and
waders that congregate in
the sheltered estuary
during the winter
months.

*The Post Office at Ferryside –
a village near the mouth of
the Tywi estuary*

Around Ferryside Walk

Allow up to 2 hours for this easy walk that gives
wonderful views over the Tywi estuary. Some of the
tracks and fields will be muddy at times.

I started this walk from a point about 1 mile outside
Ferryside but you may like to do it the other way
around particularly if you use public transport to get to
the village.

Taking care to pull in as much as possible, park on the
grass verge near the track to Is-coed Home Farm (about 1
mile outside Ferryside on the Carmarthen road).

Walk up the track until you reach the gaunt ruins of Is-coed, the former home of Sir Thomas Picton, who died at the Battle of Waterloo, and whose statue stands in the nearby town of Carmarthen. Continue past the ruins until you reach a track down to a farm. Turn left down this track and then, on reaching the farm, go over a stile opposite the farmyard. This part of the walk is now well signposted and, following the direction of the yellow arrows, bear slightly left across the field to another stile next to a gate.

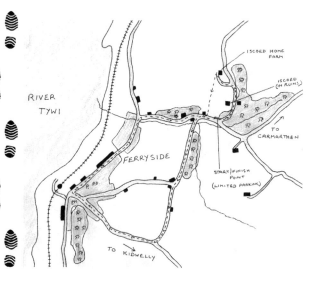

Go over the stile, then follow the hedgerow straight down through the field. Bear slightly right to cross the stile in the fence. Continue downhill heading towards woodland on the right. Now follow the woodland fence down to the stile and the gate. Cross the stile and go out onto the lane. Turn right and walk along the lane to the first turning on the left. Cross the bridge over the two streams, which form a mini waterfall where they meet.

Continue up this narrow and steep lane for approximately ½ mile to a junction. (It feels like more!) Go straight ahead to follow an even narrower lane for another third of a mile. On reaching the larger lane, turn right and follow it to Ferryside village. At the junction in the village centre (opposite the underpass to the beach and next to the car-park), turn right and remain on this road to reach the starting point of the walk in about 1 mile.

River
USK

Introduction

The River Usk is one of the best known of the South Wales rivers. It is situated between the Teifi and Tywi of West Wales and the famous Wye in the east.

The river's source is in spectacular Brecon Beacons scenery just to the north of Bannau Sir Gaer (Carmarthen Fan). It flows north to the Usk reservoir and Trecastle (Trecastell), then begins its easterly course to Brecon (Aberhonddu). Here the valley forms the northern boundary of the Brecon Beacons National Park.

From Brecon the river runs parallel to the Monmouthshire and Brecon canal and south-east to Abergavenny (Y Fenni), which is the major town on the Usk, until the river almost reaches the sea at Newport (Casnewydd).

From Trecastle, the A40 follows the river to Abergavenny. From there, good minor roads follow the river valley to the small town of Usk (Brynbuga) and down to Caerleon (Caerllion). The A449 trunk road also runs parallel to the river here. Although the noise of the traffic does disturb the peace of the valley, it provides a quick and direct route from Newport to the English Midlands.

Abergavenny is also on the railway with connections to South Wales, Bristol and Hereford. Accommodation within the National Park is varied. There are many camping and caravan sites and youth hostels at Llanddeusant in the west, near Storey Arms in the central Beacons, and north of Abergavenny in the Vale of Ewyas.

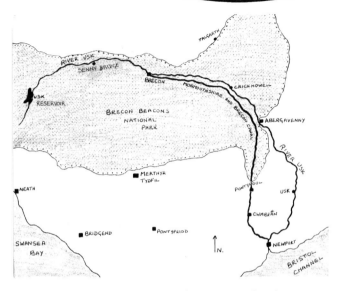

Other accommodation ranges from country hotels to farmhouse bed and breakfast.

For the more active visitor there are centres providing outdoor activities such as rock climbing, abseiling, canoeing, pot-holing and mountain biking. Several places in the Park will hire out mountain bikes on a daily or weekly basis.

OS maps covering the River Usk are 160, 161 and 171 in the Landranger 1:50,000 series. Brecon Beacons Outdoor Leisure Series 1:25,000 show much more detail and are excellent for walkers.

The Upper Reaches and the Brecon Beacons (Bannau Brycheiniog)

Nearly 1700 feet (500 metres) up in the western part of the Brecon Beacons National Park, the River Usk has its source beneath the steep cliffs of Bannau Sir Gaer and Bannau Brycheiniog with their twin lakes Llyn y Fan Fach and Llyn y Fan Fawr.

The river's watershed can be reached by taking a track south-east off the mountain road from Tal-sarn to Trecastle and 1½ miles east of Tal-sarn. Alternatively, park in the lay-by beside the first bridge over the Usk (near the Carmarthenshire county boundary sign) and walk down a fairly obvious track near the right bank of the river and head in a southerly direction. There is no public path to the river's source and, like the rest of the National Park, the land you will be crossing is private. There are many different landowners throughout the Park

River Usk at Pont ar Wysg in the Brecon Beacons

including forestry companies, the water authority, commoners' associations, and farmers. There are also some reserves and estates owned or managed by the National Trust or Countryside Council for Wales.

Walking across these mountains (particularly where there are no well-trodden paths) should only be undertaken by those properly equipped. A compass is essential – one stream or grassy ridge looks very much like the next. Weather is constantly changing and the temperature on the hills is always several degrees lower than in the valleys, even on warm summer days. Throughout the summer there are guided walks organised by the wardens from the Brecon Beacons Mountain Centre.

The Usk Reservoir and the River to Trecastle (Trecastell)

Of the many reservoirs within the National Park the Usk reservoir is one of the more recent. It was completed in 1955 and stands surrounded by commercial forestry, some of which is now being felled. The reservoir covers 290 acres and has a capacity of 2,700 million gallons with a dam 109 feet (33 metres) high. There is very good fishing and permits can be obtained from the Keeper's House on the north bank of the lake. There are several parking and picnic sites around the lake and in the forest where there are also many paths and tracks to walk.

The red soil, familiar throughout the Park and which sticks so well to shoes and boots, is old red

Usk Reservoir

sandstone, part of a ridge that stretches for fifty miles from the Tywi valley in the west.

Although generally known as the Brecon Beacons, the National Park consists of four distinct mountain ranges. From west to east they are the Black Mountain, Fforest Fawr, central Brecon Beacons (with the Park's highest peak Pen y Fan 2906 feet/886 metres), and near the border with England, the Black Mountains. The central Beacons and the eastern Black Mountains, being closer to large population centres in the South Wales valleys, are the most frequented by visitors.

South-west of Brecon, near Libanus, the Brecon Beacons Mountain Centre was opened in 1966. It stands in lonely countryside on Mynydd Illtud but is easily accessible from all areas of the Park. It is open every day except Christmas Day and gives an insight into every aspect of the Park from prehistoric times. Present day problems are those of balancing tourism with the sensitive ecology of the area and the needs of the farmers and commoners. There are picnic areas around the centre, toilets, and plenty of parking.

Trecastle and Senny Bridge
(Pontsenni)

The river Usk and A40 first meet up at the village of Trecastle, an important stopping-off place on the old mail coach road from Llandovery (Llanymddyfri). Many of the buildings in the village date back to those days. As well as the rows of houses along the main road Trecastle has some interesting back lanes to explore.

The church of this parish is one mile west at Llywel. It is situated off the A40 almost opposite the motel complex. Surrounded by ancient yews it has a battlemented tower dating from the 15th century and inside is a 16th century screen. It is dedicated to three familiar saints of Wales, David, Teilo and Padarn. The church was restored by Sir Gilbert Scott in 1869.

The castle from which Trecastle gets its name is a motte-and-bailey type dating from the 12th century. Today it is a high mound covered in mature beech trees.

A couple of miles east of Trecastle, Senny Bridge is a small town at the confluence of the rivers

Castle mound at Trecastle

Senni and Usk. There are remains of a castle but today Senny Bridge is best known as a livestock market town and home to a large army camp.

A main road leads south from Senny Bridge and forks at Defynnog, a small village with a fine church, parts of which date from the 15th century. The unusual font dates from the 12th century and has a rare Runic inscription (an ancient alphabet probably derived from Greek script and in use from about 300 AD).

In 1872 the Neath/Brecon railway arrived signalling the growth of Senny Bridge as a market town.

Aberbrân

Packhorse bridge over the Brân stream near Aberbrân

Between Senny Bridge and Brecon, two large estates can be seen from the A40 – Abercamlais and Pen-pont.

Abercamlais is down a lane off the main road opposite the turning signposted Cwm Camlais. It is a tall and quite plain house dating from the early 18th century and was home to the Williams family, another branch of which owned nearby Pen-pont. In the grounds of Abercamlais house an unusual dovecote dates from 1720. It is built of stone and has an octagonal top on a square base. It stands on a bridge over a stream.

Pen-pont House stands near the A40 and was built in 1666 for another branch of the Williams family who claimed to descend from the same line as Ann Boleyn. The house was re-fronted in 1813. From the lovely, wooded grounds came the oak beams to support Big Ben in London. Beside the road, Betws Pen-pont church was rebuilt by Sir Gilbert Scott in 1865 in the Early English style.

A little over a mile east of Pen-pont, Aberbrân Fawr is a large 16th century house near a bridge over the Usk built by James Parry in 1791. Farther down the lane opposite Aberbrân Fach farm there is a small packhorse bridge (pedestrians only) over the Brân stream.

Aberbrân Walk

A fairly gentle, level walk; allow 2-2¼ hours.

Park just over Aberbrân bridge, taking care to pull well off the road.

Continue down the lane as far as Aberbrân Fach farm. Go through the gap in the stone wall opposite the farm entrance. Go over the packhorse bridge over the Brân stream then cross the stile; the route of the footpath is now marked by yellow arrows though they do not appear very frequently.

Walk straight across the field then cross the stile in the hedgerow. Keeping the hedge on your right continue through the field. Go through a metal gate and walk ahead to the next stile in the hedge (under a large tree). Now keeping the hedge on your left follow it round to the corner of the field and go over another stile. Head across this field towards the buildings, and go over the stile on to the lane. Turn right and follow the lane for approximately ½ mile to Aberysgir bridge. Go over the stile on the right and walk beside the river. Go over the stile in the corner of the field, then go uphill through the trees and cross another stile at the top. Go straight across the field away from the woodland and on to the farm track. Turn right down the track to visit the site of the Roman fort, Y Gaer.

Return to Aberysgir bridge by the same route, turn left and walk to the hamlet of Aberysgir (¼ mile). Opposite a large, white, modern house, go down a track, go past another large house and continue as if you are going into the farmyard.

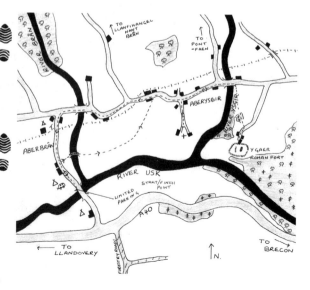

Visit Aberysgir church, which may be open. Follow the track back to the lane, turn left, and walk back to Aberbrân – about 1½ miles.

Y Gaer and the Romans

Behind a large farmhouse dating from 1900 and next to the Ysgir stream are the remains of Y Gaer. The name simply means 'the fort' and it was the largest Roman fort of its kind in Wales. It was founded in AD75 and may have been called Cicutio. Originally it was a wooden construction rebuilt of stone around AD140. It was occupied for several centuries and is on the main routes to Neath (Castell-nedd), Abergavenny and the Roman camps and fort north of the Usk reservoir near Llandovery (Llanymddyfri). The fort was excavated in 1924-25 by Sir Mortimer Wheeler and the outline and general shape of the fort can be seen. Today the field in which it stands is grazed by sheep and cows and it's a lovely peaceful spot with views of the Usk valley.

Although the fort is open for public viewing it

The Roman fort of Y Gaer near Brecon

189

may be as well to ask at the farm if you wish to visit the site. It's right at the back of the farm buildings and you will need to go through the farmyard (and several gates) to reach the fort.

The little hamlet of Aberysgir consists of a few houses, a couple of farms, and a church. The church is not even marked on some maps but it's down a small lane that looks like a private drive and does, in fact, lead into a farmyard. The church is opposite the farm buildings and dates from 1861.

Brecon (Aberhonddu)

The town of Brecon is Aberhonddu in Welsh. The name signifies its position near the confluence of the rivers Honddu and Usk. It has been an important settlement since Roman times and many artefacts dug up in the locality are displayed at the excellent Brecknock Museum. The museum is housed in the former Shire Hall – an unusual and striking Grecian style building dating from 1842.

The town centre is dominated by St Mary's church, which was restored by T.H.Wyatt and has a good 16th century tower.

Near the Honddu stream and the remains of the Benedictine priory is St John's church. It became a cathedral after the creation of the Swansea and Brecon diocese in 1923.

Overlooking the mouth of the Honddu, Brecon castle seems almost part of the Castle Hotel. The best stretch of town wall remaining is alongside the Captains Walk – so called because it was here that French officers captured during the Napoleonic wars took their exercise.

Beside the River Usk, Christ's College is one of Wales's most famous public schools. It was originally a Dominican friary founded in 1250 and then established as a college by Henry VIII in 1541. It has great sporting and academic rivalry with Llandovery College in the Tywi valley.

Today Brecon is a bustling market and tourist centre now thankfully bypassed by the A40. There is plenty of accommodation in and around the town as well as restaurants, pubs and cafés and a National Park information centre in the mart car-park.

Brecon castle

There are many riverside walks near Brecon and the town is also the starting point for the Monmouthshire and Brecon canal, which was opened in 1800 and is now so naturalised that it is more like a slow, winding river than the commercial waterway it was originally intended to be.

Brecon to Pencelli

From Brynach lock west of Brecon, two contrasting roads follow the valley of the River Usk all the way to Crickhowell (Crucywel).

The B4558 follows close to the canal whilst the main road (A40) keeps to the north of the river.

Just off the B road about 1 mile from Brynach is the quiet little village of Llanfrynach. The church is

Pencelli castle

dedicated to St Brynach and stands in well-kept grounds. The church was rebuilt in 1856 by W.Jones but the tower is much older. Inside are memorials to the de Wintons of Maesderwen, a nearby estate.

The Menascin stream flows through the village and there are several lovely stream-side and woodland walks around the village.

To the north-east of Llanfrynach and between the A40 and the River Usk is Llanhamlach – a few cottages, a hotel, a couple of farms, and down by the river, the church and rectory. To reach the church and a pleasant riverside walk, take the lane down towards the hotel then bear left following the footpath signs.

Inside the church there is an ancient stone with the words 'Johannis Moridic set up this stone' inscribed on it in Latin.

Back beside the canal the village of Pencelli used to have a stone Norman castle; now all that remains is a bramble-covered hump behind the 'new' Pencelli castle.

In the village there are camping and caravan sites, an inn, and canal boat trips are available. A side lane over the canal leads to Llanfeugan church, beautifully sited amidst ancient yews near two streams.

Pencelli Walk

Allow 3 hours; some muddy tracks.

Park in the large lay-by on the B4558 on the east side of Pencelli. Walk back towards the village and bear left along the lane off the main road. Continue until you arrive opposite the canal and then cross a stile on your left. Walk up the field beside the stream. Following the yellow arrows continue uphill. When the path becomes a track you begin to leave the stream behind. Cross a stile beneath a large tree and walk directly across the field to a gate in the hedgerow. Turn left down the farm lane and follow this for about ½ mile until you come to a T-junction. Bear left then go through the first gate on your right. Go straight ahead across the field and then bear uphill and cross a stile in the fence. Keeping along the same line and parallel to the canal below, cross several more stiles until you see ahead of you the houses of Cross Oak. Start to bear downhill and go under a line of telegraph poles. Go through the new metal gate on to the lane, and then turn right and

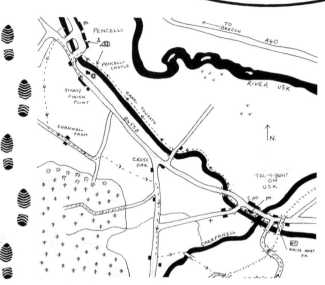

follow this lane for about a mile. Almost opposite a large farm you will see a stile in the hedge on your left. Cross the stile, go straight down the field and then cross another stile at the bottom on your left. Cross the footbridge over the river and then head straight across the field and climb the stone steps and stile in front of you. Go on to the track and under the old railway bridge and then bear left along the track away from a house in the dip. Go through a metal gate and then bear right climbing through a field and joining a muddy track half way up. Go through a gate on to a well-used track, turn left, and follow it back to the canal at Tal-y-bont. Join the canal towpath near the White Hart Inn, turn right, and follow the towpath back to Pencelli. Leave the towpath at the modern road bridge and once on the road turn left and walk back to the lay-by.

Tal-y-Bont and Llansanffraid

Tal-y-bont on Usk lies beside the Monmouthshire and Brecon canal and the Caerfanell stream. Beside the stream is the course of an old tramroad that preceded the Brecon and Merthyr railway whose bridge over the road near the village still remains.

South of Tal-y-bont, a reservoir of the same name is surrounded by conifers where there are parking places and picnic sites and many public footpaths. A popular waymarked route for cyclists as well as walkers is the Taff Trail, which follows the tramroad down beside the lake.

Tal-y-bont is probably the most popular village on the canal and as such gets very crowded in summer. It's a well established mooring point for canal-boats and caters for visitors with two inns and a well-stocked shop.

Across the Usk and beside the A40, Llansan-ffraid church is the burial place of Henry Vaughan. He was born in 1621 at Newton, a farmhouse

Monmouthshire and Brecon canal

about a mile along the road towards Brecon. He spent most of his life at Newton writing poetry and practising

medicine until his death in 1695. The church by
S.W.Williams dates from 1885.

A few miles north of Llansanffraid, Llangorse Lake
(Llyn Syfaddan) is the second largest natural lake in
Wales (the largest is Llyn Tegid or Bala Lake on the
Dee). Although at one time peaceful it is now so
popular that in summer it can be difficult to find a
quiet spot. There are plenty of parking and picnic sites,
and camping and caravanning facilities are available. A
particularly nice walk is from the car-park on the north-
west side of the lake to Llangasty church and cottages
on the southern side.

Llanddeti and Llangynidr

River Usk at Llangynidr bridge

Just beyond Tal-y-bont
the canal and River
Usk meet up and
continue side by side
towards Crickhowell.

Llanddeti church
stands above the winding,
high-banked river. In
Cromwell's time, the
church was used as a farm
building by the Puritan
Col Jenkins Jones whose
home was nearby
Llanddeti Hall.

Along the river,
Llangynidr is a village in
two parts.

Upper Llangynidr has an inn, canal boat trips, and
scores of visitors. Down a narrow lane, Lower
Llangynidr has a six-arched bridge over the Usk that
dates from 1600. There are lovely riverside walks from
the bridge. North of Llangynidr, the village of Bwlch is
situated on a sharp bend of the A40 where a road goes
north to Talgarth. The main road here is squeezed
between the hills (hence the village's name, which means
'pass') and is on the line of the Roman road. About a
mile due east, a Roman fort sits beside a farmhouse.

Just to the east of Llangynidr a road runs south
across the mountain and in a few miles you leave behind
the peaceful, wooded Usk valley for the outer reaches of
industrial South Wales.

Mynydd Llangynidr and its neighbour, Mynydd
Llangatwg, rise above the Usk valley to the south. A
feature of these hills is the limestone crags and cliffs and
at Craig y Cilau, south-west of Crickhowell, there is a
National Nature Reserve with some public access.

Llangynidr Walk

A fairly easy walk that can be muddy. Allow up to 2
hours.

Park in Lower Llangynidr near the telephone box.
Walk down the hill towards the bridge over the Usk.
Before crossing the bridge go down the worn footpath
on your right. Follow the narrow path along the bank of
the river and continue for about 1 mile. In places the
path climbs up into the woods and if the river is in
flood you will have to find a higher path but always
keep parallel to the river. When the path eventually

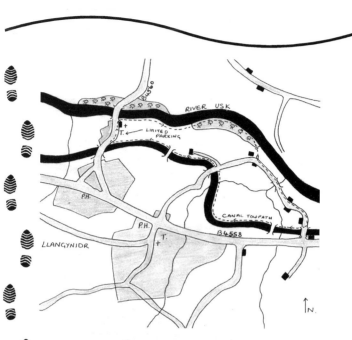

peters out you will see some steps leading uphill away
from the river. Go up these steps and follow the worn
path next to a stone wall round and up on to a narrow
lane. Turn left and continue for about ¼ mile until you
reach a bridge over the canal. Go down on to the
towpath, turn right, and follow it back to Llangynidr.
At the modern road bridge leave the towpath and turn
right to get back to the telephone box.

Tretower (Tretûr) and Crickhowell (Crucywel)

Tretower Court and Castle stand near the Rhiangoll stream about 2½ miles north-west of Crickhowell.

The castle remains consist of a tall, circular 13th century tower and an earlier keep. Tretower Court dates from the 14th and 15th centuries with later additions. It is built around a courtyard and exceptionally well preserved. Between the 15th and 18th centuries it was occupied by the Vaughans after which it became a farm. In 1930 it was sensitively restored by the Ministry of Works and today it attracts large numbers of visitors. Near the court, Tretower church was built in 1877 by Sir Joseph Bailey, lord of the nearby Glan Usk Park.

Table Mountain near Crickhowell

Crickhowell takes its name from a hilltop cairn above the town – *crug* Hywel. It is set on top of the conspicuous and aptly named Table Mountain, which rises to 1480 feet (451 metres). Crickhowell town has buildings dating from the 13th century. The oldest is Alisby's Castle, which was built in 1272. Today the grounds surrounding the ruins are a public park. It was built for Sir Grimbald Pauncefort but changed hands several times. Its name derives from an ally of one-time owner, Roger Mortimer. Alisby secured Mortimer's release from the Tower of London and received the castle as a gift of thanks.

Beside the A40, near the junction with New Road, Porth Mawr was the gateway to a large house (now demolished) called Cwrt y Carw, which was built in Henry VIII's time and was home to the Herbert family.

Crickhowell bridge is unusual in that it appears to have 13 arches on one side and only 12 on the other. It was rebuilt in 1706 but the 'odd' arch is due to alterations in 1830.

Abergavenny (Y Fenni)

Abergavenny has long been known as 'the Gateway to Wales' and is situated just outside the eastern boundary of the Brecon Beacons National Park where the River Usk begins its southward journey to Newport and the sea.

The town is surrounded by memorable, walkable hills, three of which are within the National Park boundary. Probably best known and most popular of these is the Sugar Loaf to the north-west of the town. It rises to 1955 feet (596 metres) and there are footpaths up to the summit from all directions. The shortest walk up to the top of the hill is from the viewpoint car-park near the ridge of Mynydd Llanwenarth. From here it's just over a mile and a half to the summit.

South of Abergavenny, the Blorenge rises to 1833 feet (559 metres) and can be reached from the minor road off the B4246 Govilon to Blaenafon road.

To the east of Abergavenny are the twin hills, Ysgyryd Fawr and Ysgyryd Fach. Both provide good viewpoints over the town and surrounding countryside. Like the Sugar Loaf, Ysgyryd Fawr is owned by the National Trust and there are several paths up to the hill.

River Usk near Abergavenny

Market day in Abergavenny sees the town packed with locals and tourists attracted from a wide area of South-East Wales. For visitors the town has an information centre and is a popular base for those keen on an 'outdoor' holiday: walkers, fishermen, pony-trekkers and, of course, canal enthusiasts. Govilon wharf just south of the town is a favourite place to 'pick up' the canal and there are boat trips from here.

Abergavenny Walk

A gentle riverside stroll; allow 1½–1¾ hours. From the town centre take the road signposted to Pontypridd and, after crossing the Usk, continue to a large lay-by on your left where you can leave the car. Walk back across the bridge and go down the steps on your left. Continue beside the river, go over the stile next to the metal gate, and walk along the worn path between the wood and the river. Bear left to cross the footbridge over the stream and then continue beside the

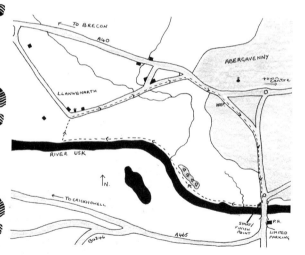

river. Cross another wooden footbridge and continue straight on. After three more stiles turn right and follow the fence away from the riverbank towards the houses. Continue as far as the lane, cross the stile, and turn right (Llanwenarth church is on the left). Follow this lane, and at the first junction bear right to join the main road (A40). Walk along the road until just past the hospital, turn right, and continue to the next main road. Turn right and walk back to the Usk bridge.

Abergavenny to Usk (Brynbuga)

From Abergavenny, the A40 continues in an easterly direction for Monmouth (Trefynwy) and Ross on Wye (Y Gelli Gandryll). The River Usk and the canal flow south and if you join the B4598 from the A465/ A40 interchange you can follow the river to the small town of Usk.

Soon you leave behind the mountains of Wales and the River Usk meanders through the rich farmland of Monmouthshire.

South of Abergavenny, Llanofer House was home in the 19th century to Lady Llanofer a champion of Welsh language and tradition. She was the founder of the Welsh Manuscript Society and as a teetotaller bought up

Llancaeo windmill

203

many local inns and turned them into coffee houses. Near the village of Llanvihangel Gobion (Llanfihangel-y-gofion) and on the east bank of the Usk, are the wooded grounds of Clytha Park (Cleidda). The entrance arch was built by William Jones in 1790 and the house begun in 1824 to designs by Edward Haycock. Occasionally the grounds are open to the public. Nearby Clytha Castle is a folly built in 1790 also by William Jones in memory of his wife. The estate is owned by the National Trust who have passed the folly over to the Landmark Trust who rent it out for holiday accommodation.

South of Clytha, Coed y Bonedd (Wood of the Gentry) is a good example of an Iron Age hill-fort. It is also owned by the National Trust and footpaths lead up to the woods surrounding the fort.

The B4598 crosses the Usk at Chain Bridge – rebuilt in 1906 with iron girders rather than chains. A narrow lane leads off the main road opposite the inn, and in less than a mile, reaches the village of Betws Newydd whose outskirts have been rather spoilt by new developments. Nearby is the large Alice Springs golf-course.

Back on the main road to Usk, Llancaeo windmill stands ruined and gaunt in the centre of the Usk valley.

Betws Newydd Walk

Mostly level walking; allow up to 2 hours. Park in Betws Newydd wherever possible. Walk up the lane towards the Chain Bridge. Continue for approximately 1 mile until you reach a footpath and the Usk Valley

Walk signpost on the right next to a wood. Go over the
stile and walk down a worn path through the wood
above the River Usk. Following the path and the yellow
waymarks, continue parallel to the river for
approximately 1 mile crossing stiles and walking
through fields, parkland, and along tracks. Be sure to

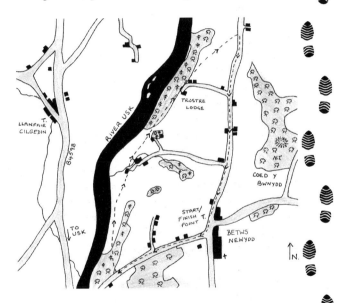

keep to the route shown by the waymarkers as some
parts of the Usk Valley Way are not public footpaths but
permissive paths and are as private as a back garden.

    Just after crossing the track to Trostre Lodge, the
waymarked path continues beside the river and through
a wood. Here you should continue straight ahead, cross
a stile, and start to veer away from the river. Crossing a
small stream and keeping the wood on your left, climb

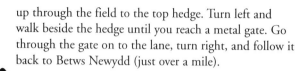

up through the field to the top hedge. Turn left and walk beside the hedge until you reach a metal gate. Go through the gate on to the lane, turn right, and follow it back to Betws Newydd (just over a mile).

Usk (Brynbuga)

The town of Usk lies on the east bank of the river and has been a settlement since Roman times. The Roman station was called Burrium and was built at the time of Claudius and then rebuilt in about AD65.

The town has a ruined medieval castle that is still in private hands and not generally open to the public.

Usk's church was originally built as a priory for

Benedictine nuns and inside are some good examples of church woodwork including a screen of English design.

The town's clock tower dates from 1887.

Usk is best known today for its excellent fishing and the nearby agricultural college. According to legend, King Arthur caught salmon in the Usk near the town and served it up at his Round Table.

In an old malt barn near the town centre is

The clock tower, Usk

the fascinating Gwent Museum of Rural Life open throughout the year. The narrow bridge over the Usk was rebuilt in 1836.

East of Usk and beside the busy A449, Llangeview (Llangyfiw) church stands in a pleasant, grassy churchyard but unfortunately the almost constant drone from the nearby trunk road spoils the once peaceful situation.

Farther south, two villages look at each other across the Usk valley. On the west side, Llangybi consists of a group of old houses and a large church in the perpendicular style. North of the village is the drive to Llangibby castle, a large 18th century house demolished in 1950. On the hilltop beyond are the remains of the original castle, dating from Norman times, that was never completed and played no part in the history of Monmouthshire. Llantrisant near the east bank of the Usk is a quiet village with a good riverside inn.

Newbridge on Usk Walk

A fairly easy walk with a couple of minor hills but may be muddy in places; you should allow up to 2 hours.

Park in the lay-by just east of Newbridge, walk back towards the village, and cross the bridge over the Usk. Walk up the hill past the inn, then just on the corner go over a stile on the left. Cross diagonally to the next stile, then go straight across the field towards a house. Cross the stile next to a metal gate and turn left down towards the buildings. Walk between the houses, and then bear right; cross a stream and go through a metal gate. Walk straight uphill through the field heading towards the top

right-hand corner and cross a stile. Go straight down
the field towards a row of trees, through a gate, and

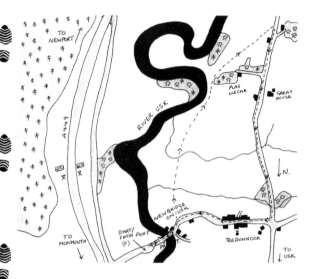

then cross a stream. Walk uphill through the field then
down under a large tree; bear right and then go through
a metal gate near the top right-hand corner of the field.
Go through a gap and then begin to bear down towards
the bank of the River Usk. Turn towards a row of
conifers, go over the fence into a wood and then straight
ahead and over a stile. Keeping the wood on your left,
walk uphill close to the fence and then continue to skirt
the wood until you reach a metal gate on the left. Do
not go through the gate; rather bear right uphill towards
a gap in the hedge. Climb the fence and then head
across the field towards the farm buildings. Keeping the
farm on your right bear left, go through a metal gate,

and then cross a stile. Go diagonally across this field, cross the farm track, and go over a stile into another field. Continue straight ahead through the field, then cross a stile onto a lane. Turn right and follow this lane for about 1¼ miles to a cross-roads. Turn right, and follow this busier road back to Newbridge – 1 mile.

The Usk Valley to Caerleon (Caerllion)

In the days of river commerce, Newbridge on Usk was the highest point to which barges could sail. Here the Usk becomes tidal and flooding can occur at any time of the year. Often the valley floor is strewn with material deposited by the receding floodwaters, everything from plastic bottles to logs and branches.

The 'new bridge' was built in 1779 and the little hamlet named after it has a welcoming inn.

Just along the lane, Tredynog is a peaceful little village with a church restored in 1910. It has tiny Norman windows in the chancel and a stone font dating from 1662.

Tredynog church

A stone dating from the 2nd century has an inscription recalling the burial of Julianus, a soldier of the second legion. It was found in the churchyard and is now set above the font. A mile south of Newbridge, near the A449 picnic sites, there is a motte-and-bailey castle overlooking the river and another mile farther south are the forlorn ruins of Kemeys (Cemais) Inferior church.

One of the best ways to explore the countryside and villages near the River Usk is to follow the Usk Valley Walk. This is a continuous waymarked walk following over 25 miles of the river valley from Caerleon to just outside Abergavenny. Yellow dots and yellow arrows on a black background (on wooden posts or footpath signs) are regular throughout the walk, so it should be quite easy to follow. Not all the walk is along public rights of way; some of it crosses private farmland or woodland and access is only possible with the co-operation of the landowners. The walk follows lanes and tracks and takes you through villages and farmsteads and sometimes right beside or above the river bank. The Betws Newydd walk in this chapter follows part of the Usk Valley Walk.

Caerleon (Caerllion)

The name Caerleon means 'the camp of the legions' and it was here that the Romans had their military and civilian settlement, although the large civilian settlement was at Caer-went, north of Caldicot.

The camp dates from AD74 or 75 and was built as a permanent fortress for the second Augustinian Legion (5,600 troops). Some of the Roman town now lies under modern housing but remains that can still be seen include the baths, barrack block, and the amphitheatre. These were excavated by Sir Mortimer Wheeler in the 1920s.

In the town there is a museum filled with Roman artefacts.

Caerleon's bridge over the Usk dates from 1806 and replaces an earlier bridge farther upstream, probably near the site of the Roman bridge.

In the town centre, two inns stand opposite each other; both have 16th century windows. The parish church is dedicated to St Cadog and was largely restored in 1867 but retains a fine Norman arch incorporated in the south wall.

To the north-east, the town is overlooked by a hill-fort and beside a tributary of the Usk is the site of a Civil War fort. Both can be reached by public footpaths from near the town.

St Cadog's church, Caerleon

Although managing to preserve the old world charm in the town centre, Caerleon today is under tremendous pressure from nearby Newport (Casnewydd). New housing estates crowd most of the hillsides surrounding the town.

Newport (Casnewydd) and the River Estuary

In the 19th century Newport's importance grew as a port for the export of iron, steel and, of course, coal from the surrounding valleys of South-East Wales.

Industry and agriculture share the Gwent levels east of Newport

Among the buildings recalling earlier times is the castle beside the River Usk, which was founded by Robert Fitzhamon in 1171. It survived intact until the 14th century when it was remodelled. The central tower contained a chapel and below was a water gate.

Originally Newport was Casnewydd ar Wysg (Newcastle on Usk) and only as it grew became Newport to distinguish it from the old town of Caerleon.

On Stow Hill, St Woolos' Church became the cathedral for the diocese of Monmouth in 1921. It has a good Norman doorway.

Another old building in Newport is Murenger House dating from Tudor times. Most of the rest of the town's architecture dates from the 19th and 20th centuries. There is a very good museum, an art gallery, and an information centre.

Over the river to the east of the town are the giant Llan-wern steel works and, south of Newport, the Usk marshes are shared by agriculture and industry. Minor roads lead to pleasant little villages like Goldcliff and Nash. The flat lands are intersected by drainage ditches giving more of a feel of the Somerset levels or Romney marsh – except for the huge chimneys and pylons.

Despite this, the marshland villages do have a charm and the Gwent Wildlife Trust (Head Office in Church Street, Monmouth) own stretches of the marshes between Goldcliff and Magor Pill and west of Newport near Peterstone Wentloog (Llan-bedr Gwynllŵg). The Trust has many other reserves in the county. Another one on the Usk is Priory Wood near Betws Newydd.

We publish a variety of books about Wales, the Welsh language, and Welsh politics. For a full list of publications, send now for your FREE copy of our new, full-colour Catalogue – or simply surf into it on the Word Wide Web!

TALYBONT CEREDIGION CYMRU SY24 5HE
e-bost ylolfa@ylolfa.com
y we http://www.ylolfa.com/
ffôn (01970) 832 304
ffacs & ISDN 832 782